Children with Visual Impairment in Mainstream Settings

Children with Visual Impairment in Mainstream Settings

Christine Arter, Heather L. Mason, Steve McCall, Mike McLinden and Juliet Stone

David Fulton Publishers
London

David Fulton Publishers Ltd
Ormond House, 26–27 Boswell Street, London WC1N 3JZ

www.fultonpublishers.co.uk

First published in Great Britain by David Fulton Publishers 1999
Reprinted 2001

Note: The rights of Christine Arter, Heather Mason, Steve McCall, Mike McLinden and
Juliet Stone to be identified as the authors of this work have been asserted by them in
accordance with the Copyright, Designs and Patents Act 1988.

Copyright © David Fulton Publishers 1999

British Library Cataloguing in Publication Data
A catalogue record for this book is available from the British Library

ISBN 1–85346–583–6

Typeset by Saxon Graphics Ltd, Derby.
Printed in Great Britain by The Cromwell Press Ltd, Trowbridge, Wilts.

Contents

Foreword

Each publication in this series of books is concerned with approaches to intervention with children with specific needs in mainstream schools. In this preface we provide a backdrop of general issues concerning special needs in mainstream schools. The government's recent Action Programme, published after considering responses to the Special Educational Needs (SEN) Green Paper, will lead to changes in practice in the future. Following consultation, there will be a revised and simplified Code of Practice in place by the school year 2000/2001. It is intended that this will make life easier.

The SEN Code of Practice (DfE 1994a), following the 1993 Education Act, provides practical guidance to LEAs and school governing bodies on their responsibilities towards pupils with SEN. Schools and LEAs were required to regard its recommendations from September 1994. The Department for Education also issued Circular 6/94 (DfE 1994b) which provided suggestions as to how schools should manage their special needs provision alongside that made by other local schools. These documents embody the twin strategies of individual pupil support and whole-school development. The Green Paper *Excellence for All* also seeks to promote the development of more sophisticated and comprehensive forms of regional and local planning (DfEE 1997).

The Code of Practice, with its staged approach to assessment supervised within each mainstream school by a teacher designated as Special Educational Needs Coordinator (SENCO), was widely welcomed.

For example, Walters (1994) argued that 'this Code of Practice builds on good practice developed over the ten years and heralds a "new deal" for children with special needs in the schools of England and Wales'. But he also reflected worries that, in the light of other developments, the process might provide an added incentive for schools to dump their 'problem children into the lap of the LEA' rather than devising strategies to improve behaviour in the school environment. Such children, he feared, were in danger of being increasingly marginalised.

Impact on teachers

While receiving a mainly positive welcome for its intentions, the Code of Practice (DfE 1994a) also raised some concerns about its impact on teachers who became responsible for its implementation. On the positive side the Code would raise the profile of special needs and establish a continuum of provision in mainstream schools. There was a clear specification of different types of special educational need and the Code's emphasis was on meeting them through individual programmes developed in cooperation with parents.

However, there were possible problems in meeting the challenge of establishing effective and time-efficient procedures for assessment and monitoring. Further challenges were to be found in making best use of resources and overcoming barriers to liaison with parents.

Anxieties about the Code

Following the introduction of the Code these anxieties were confirmed by a number of research studies of teachers' perceptions of the impact of the Code. The picture which emerged from these studies showed appreciation of the potential benefits of implementing the Code but widespread anxiety, based on early experience, about the practicalities of making it work.

Loxley and Bines (1995) interviewed head teachers and SENCOs about their views on emergent issues related to the complexities of introducing Individual Education Plans (IEPs), particularly in secondary schools.

Teachers feared that 'excessive proceduralism' could lead to the distribution of resources being skewed towards meeting the needs of children whose parents are best able to understand and exercise their rights, at the expense of provision for children whose parents are less assertive and confident. Teachers were most concerned about the allocation of scarce resources and the increased responsibilities of SENCOs for managing a system likely to reduce time for direct teaching of children.

School perspectives

Most schools were optimistic about their ability to implement the Code and positive about LEA guidelines and training, but there was less certainty that the Code would improve the education of pupils with SEN.

Asked to give their opinion on advantages and disadvantages of the Code, teachers cited as positive effects:

- a more structured framework,
- growing awareness of accountability,
- a higher profile for SEN issues,
- earlier identification,
- greater uniformity in practice, and
- increased parental involvement.

The disadvantages cited were:

- lack of resources and time,
- substantially increased workloads for all teachers as well as SENCOs,
- more time used for liaison and less for teaching.

(Rhodes, 1996)

Four themes

A national survey commissioned by the National Union of Teachers (NUT) identified four themes:

1. broad support for the principles and establishment of the Code of Practice;
2. concern about the feasibility of its implementation, given a lack of time and resources;
3. problems in some areas related to perceived inadequacy of LEA support;
4. inadequate status and lack of recognition for the SENCO role.

(Lewis *et al.*, 1996)

Another study found patchy support for SENCOs. There were wide variations in the amount of time dedicated to the role, the amount of support from head teachers and governors, involvement in decision-making, the extent of training and the degree of bureaucracy within LEAs.

SEN Register and Staged Assessment Procedures

Although its widespread adoption makes it appear to have been a national prescription, the five-stage model suggested in the Code is not a legal requirement. The Code actually states that: 'to give specific help to children who have special educational needs, schools should adopt a staged response'. (DfE 1994a, 2.20)

It goes on to indicate that some schools and LEAs may adopt different models but that, while it was not essential that there should be five stages, it was essential that there should be differentiation between the stages, aimed at matching action taken to the pupil's needs at each stage.

Five Key Stages

Nonetheless, the normal expectation is that assessment and intervention will be organised and recorded in an SEN Register for which the SENCO is responsible. The following description briefly summarises usual practice, with Stages 1–3 school-based and Stages 4 and 5 the responsibility of the LEA.

Stage 1

Class teacher identifies pupils with learning difficulty and, with support from the SENCO, attempts to meet the pupil's SEN.

Stage 2

Class teacher reports continued concern and SENCO takes responsibility for the special response to meet the pupil's SEN.

Stage 3

SENCO organises support from external agencies to help in meeting the pupil's SEN.

Stage 4

The LEA is approached by the school with a request for statutory assessment.

Stage 5

The LEA considers the need for a Statement of SEN and completes the assessment procedure; monitoring and review of the statement is organised by the LEA.

Each book in this series explains how this process works in relation to different disabilities and difficulties as they were described in the 1981 Act and shows how individual needs can be identified and met through IEPs. While forthcoming revision of the Code may alter the details of the stages, the principles of the practices through which needs are specified will remain the same.

Information for colleagues, governors and parents

Ensuring that the school provides all necessary information for staff, governors and parents is another major element of the SENCO role. *The Organisation of Special Educational Provision* (Circular 6/94) (DfE 1994b) sets out the issues which the school should address about its SEN provision, policies and partnerships with bodies beyond the school.

This is information that must be made available and may be found in school brochures or prospectuses, in annual reports to parents and in policy documents. The ultimate responsibility for following the guidance in the Circular rests with the head teacher and governing body but the SENCO will be engaged with all these issues. Effectively, the Circular forms a useful checklist for monitoring the development and implementation of the SEN policy.

You may find it useful to consider the following points as a way of familiarising yourself with provision in your school.

Basic information about your school's special educational provision

- Who is responsible for coordinating the day-to-day provision of education for pupils with SEN at your school (whether or not the person is known as the SEN Coordinator).
- Arrangements need to be made for coordinating the provision of education for pupils with SEN. Does your school's SENCO work alone or is there a coordinating or support team?
- What are the admission arrangements for pupils with SEN who do not have a statement and is there any priority for SEN admissions ?
- What kind of provision does your school have for the special educational needs in which it specialises?
- What are your school's access arrangements for pupils with physical and sensory disabilities?

Information about the school's policies for the identification, assessment and provision for all pupils with SEN

- What is your school policy on allocation of money for SEN resources?
- How are pupils with SEN identified and their needs determined and reviewed? How are parents told about this?
- What does your school policy say about arrangements for providing access for pupils with SEN to a balanced and broadly-based curriculum (including the National Curriculum)?
- What does your school policy say about 'integration arrangements'? How do pupils with SEN engage in the activities of the school together with pupils who do not have special educational needs?
- How does your school demonstrate the effective implementation of its SEN policy? How does the governing body evaluate the success of the education which is provided at the school for pupils with SEN?
- What are the arrangements made by the governing body relating to the treatment of complaints from parents of pupils with SEN concerning the provision made at the school?
- What are your school's 'time targets' for response to complaints?

Information about the school's staffing policies and partnership with bodies beyond the school

- What is your school's policy on continuing in-service professional training for staff in relation to special educational needs?
- What are your school's arrangements regarding the use of teachers and facilities from outside the school, including links with support services for special educational needs?
- What is the role played by the parents of pupils with SEN? Is there a 'close working relationship'?
- Do you have any links with other schools, including special schools, and is there provision made for the transition of pupils with SEN between schools or between the school and the next stage of life or education?
- How well does 'liaison and information exchange' work in your school, e.g. links with health services, social services and educational welfare services and any voluntary organisations which work on behalf of children with SEN?

In any school those arrangements which are generally available to meet children's learning needs will have an impact on those services which are required to meet specific needs. It is therefore very important that a reader of any one of this series of specialist books makes reference to the general situation in their school when thinking about ways of improving the learning situation for pupils.

Harry Daniels and Colin Smith
The University of Birmingham
February 1999

References

Crowther, D., Dyson, A. *et al.* (1997) *Implementation of the Code of Practice: The Role of the Special Educational Needs Coordinator.* Special Needs Research Centre, Department of Education, University of Newcastle upon Tyne.

Department for Education (DfE) (1994a) *Code of Practice on the Identification and Assessment of Special Educational Needs.* London: HMSO.

Department for Education (DfE) (1994b) *The Organisation of Special Educational Provision.* Circular 6/94. London: HMSO.

Department for Education and Employment (DfEE) (1997) *Excellence for All: Meeting Special Educational Needs.* London: HMSO.

Hornby, G. (1995) 'The Code of Practice: boon or burden', *British Journal of Special Education* 22(3) 116–119.

Lewis, A., Neill, S. R. St J. and Campbell, R. J. (1996) *The Implementation of the Code of Practice in Primary and Secondary School: A National Survey of the Perceptions of Special Educational Needs Coordinators.* The University of Warwick.

Loxley, A. and Bines, H. (1995) 'Implementing the Code of Practice: professional responses', *Support for Learning* 10(4) 185–189.

Rhodes, L. W. (1996) 'Code of Practice: first impressions', *Special!* Spring 1996.

Walters, B. (1994) *Management of Special Needs.* London: Cassell.

Contributors

Christine Arter

Christine Arter is a Lecturer in Special Education (Visual Impairment) at the University of Birmingham. She has had extensive teaching experience in mainstream schools and at a Birmingham school for children with a visual impairment. She is the VIEW (formerly the Association for the Education and Welfare of the Visually Impaired) representative on the RNIB Executive Council and Education and Employment Committee as well as a School Governor and a trained OFSTED Inspector. Christine is currently carrying out research in the area of Braille dyslexia.

Heather Mason

Heather Mason is Senior Lecturer in Special Education (Visual Impairment) at the University of Birmingham. Previously she worked both in mainstream education and at Priestley Smith School, Birmingham. She works extensively overseas and is an OFSTED inspector. Her PhD thesis developed a new assessment tool for blind pupils, the STIP (Speed of Tactile Information Processing).

Steve McCall

Steve McCall is a Lecturer in Special Education (Visual Impairment) at the School of Education, University of Birmingham. He worked as a class teacher at St Vincent's School for the Visually Impaired in Liverpool and as an advisory teacher for the visually impaired on the Isle of Wight. He is a member of the Braille Authority of the UK (BAUK). His research interests include the development of literacy through touch for children who have a visual impairment in combination with additional difficulties.

Mike McLinden

Mike McLinden is a Lecturer in Special Education (Visual Impairment) at the University of Birmingham with special responsibility for multiple disabilities and visual impairment. He has worked with a range of pupils with special educational needs including Emotional and Behavioural Difficulties (EBD), Moderate Learning Difficulties (MLD) and visual impairment. Mike worked as Research Fellow at the University of Birmingham on the Moon as a Route to Literacy Project and helped in the development of a variety of teaching resources for Moon.

Juliet Stone

Juliet was a former Lecturer in Special Education (Visual Impairment) at the School of Education, University of Birmingham. She is an OFSTED inspector, a trained mobility specialist and has worked extensively abroad. She was a Senior Advisory Teacher in Gloucester with responsibility for pupils with visual impairments. Her publications include *Mobility for Special Needs*.

With thanks to Lin Walsh for editing and formatting the text.

CHAPTER 1

Introduction

This book seeks to inform teachers in mainstream schools and colleges, who are new to teaching children and young people with a visual impairment, how successful inclusion may be achieved. The text will examine some of the challenges facing this group in accessing the curriculum and suggest ways in which these challenges can be met. While the book is primarily aimed at newly qualified teachers working in a mainstream school setting, it is felt that the issues raised will be of interest to all teachers who are teaching pupils with a visual impairment for the first time. Many of the more general principles will be useful to those working in further education settings. The reader will be directed to additional sources which provide greater in-depth coverage of the issues raised in this introductory text.

Incidence of visual impairment

Many teachers will have taught pupils who wear glasses to correct their vision, but few teachers will have met children and young people with poor vision that cannot be corrected with glasses, and who may be said to be visually impaired. Recent research (Clunies-Ross and Franklin 1997) suggests that there are 2.1 children per 1,000 with a visual impairment. It remains quite a rarity to find a child who is blind in a mainstream classroom and within each year-group of children in Britain, there are likely to be approximately 70 children who use Braille, and may therefore be considered educationally blind. This suggests that across the country there are about 840 children between the ages of 4 and 16 years who use Braille amounting to less than 5 per cent of all children (approximately 20,000) with a visual impairment. The research found that of primary aged children with a visual impairment, some 59 per cent attend mainstream schools, and only 7 per cent attend a special school for the visually impaired. For secondary age pupils 46 per cent attend mainstream schools, with a further 13 per cent attending a special school for the visually impaired. This research clearly demonstrates that the majority of pupils with a visual impairment are being educated in mainstream school settings.

The figures cited do not include all of those children who attend special schools, other than those designated as schools for the visually impaired. A significant proportion of children with a visual impairment have additional difficulties and are currently being educated within a range of special school settings, such as those for pupils with severe learning difficulties (SLD). It is unlikely that teachers in mainstream settings will currently be expected to teach pupils with more severe learning difficulties, although recent government policies, which recognise the entitlement of all children to be included within mainstream settings, suggest that this situation may change. Pupils with a visual impairment in combination with additional difficulties may therefore increasingly be included within mainstream settings as part of their educational placement. For these reasons this book includes a chapter addressing the needs of this particular group of pupils.

Definition of terms

Mason (1997) suggests that the World Health Organization (WHO) definition of terms are now the most widely accepted and these are based on visual acuity scores. Those with visual acuity scores ranging from:

6/6 to 6/18 may be described as having Normal vision,

<6/18 to >3/60 may be described as having Low vision,

<3/60 may be described as Blind.

Figure 1.1 illustrates the terminology used throughout this text and gives some indication of the different levels of visual functioning. For further information about levels of visual functioning, and an explanation of the acuity scores, the reader should refer to Chapter 1.

The reader will note that throughout the book the writers refer to 'the child with a visual impairment' and 'the child who is blind'. Although the phrasing sometimes appears a little clumsy, it rightly places the emphasis on the child first and not on the disability. The overall term 'visual impairment' covers a wide spectrum, and care must be taken to avoid adopting a stereotypical view of all of those who have impaired vision. The different eye conditions referred to throughout the text are highlighted in bold print, and an explanation of the terms is included in a glossary at the end of the book.

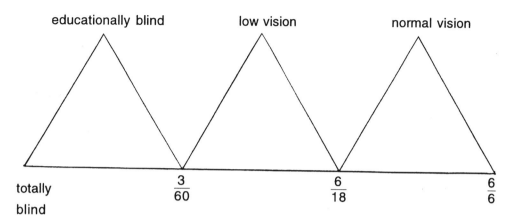

Figure 1.1 Definition of terms

Support for pupils with a visual impairment and their teachers

Pupils with a visual impairment may have complex needs, and it is the role of the teacher to ensure that they have full access to the curriculum, allowing them to achieve their full potential. Solutions to these challenges are not always simple. Wearing glasses or using enlarged print material will not necessarily meet the child's needs. For example, for those pupils with tunnel vision, perhaps as the result of **retinitis pigmentosa**, enlarging their work will mean that they can actually see less at each fixation.

Each pupil will face individual challenges when accessing the curriculum, and even those pupils with the same eye condition may present varying symptoms which require different approaches. The particular challenges experienced by any one child may also change from day to day. Variations in levels of sunlight, or even fatigue, may well affect the pupil's ability to see from one day to the next.

The pupil with visual impairment may have to work much harder than peers who are fully sighted to keep up with lessons and to achieve a comparable standard. For example, it may take the pupil with low vision much longer to read texts and to complete written work. Visual fatigue may result from the unusual working position that they are forced to adopt to see printed material or from the use of low vision aids (LVAs) such as a telescope. Many pupils with a visual impairment find it difficult to read their own handwriting when checking and redrafting work. As a consequence of their visual condition, such pupils may also have additional curricular areas and other skills to master. These may include:

- orientation and mobility skills;
- listening skills;

- using a range of adaptive technology;
- learning through touch using Braille and other tactile codes and materials;
- learning how to use their residual vision to maximum effect;
- using low vision aids such as magnifiers effectively.

Time has to be found within the already crowded school timetable to complete their work in the least stressful way and to allow the mastery of a range of skills specific to these special curricular areas.

The child with a visual impairment in a mainstream classroom is the responsibility of the class teacher. The school Special Educational Needs Coordinator (SENCO) will provide support and guidance in line with the Code of Practice (DfE 1994). More specific support may be obtained from a qualified teacher of the visually impaired who may be working in an advisory or support capacity. There are different ways in which support can be provided in schools:

- on a regular basis from the LEA peripatetic/advisory services – such teachers will usually be qualified teachers of the visually impaired;
- by a qualified teacher of the visually impaired employed by the school to provide in-class support for a number of pupils;
- in a Unit/Resource Base for the visually impaired attached to the school;
- by a Learning Support Assistant appointed to work alongside an individual pupil.

Specialist teachers of the visually impaired may work alongside the pupil to make sure that the special curriculum areas such as orientation and mobility and communication skills are covered, but they will also work directly with teachers in order to increase their level of skill and confidence. Aspects of their role may include:

Direct support for teachers

- explaining the effects of visual impairment, and how it can affect the child's daily functioning, to individual teachers or to the whole school, through in-service training;
- assessing the child's needs and advising the class/subject teachers on setting objectives and planning individual educational plans (IEPs);
- advising on:
  - resource materials, e.g. large print, raised work surfaces, low vision aids and devices (LVA/Ds), personal computers;
  - positioning of the child in the classroom and lighting conditions;
- liaising with external examination boards for additional time and resources;
- advanced preparation of materials, e.g. tactile diagrams, enlarged/adapted print copies;
- working with parents and other agencies involved.

Direct support for pupils

- assessing visual functioning and providing training in the use of residual vision including visual discrimination and perception;
- monitoring visual conditions and if necessary, referring the child to other agencies, e.g. Low Vision Clinic;
- helping with:
  - organisational and study skills;
  - acceptance of impairment, social skills, self-confidence and independence;
- developing:
  - tactile and other sensory skills to complement vision;
  - communication skills including listening, Braille and print reading, spelling and writing and keyboard skills;
  - orientation and mobility skills within the school;
  - LVA user skills.

If there is a Resource Base within the school then the pupils may attend discrete lessons to develop particular skills which need to be acquired quickly to enable inclusion. The mastery of some new piece of technological equipment or the development of Braille literacy skills when eyesight is rapidly deteriorating are two common examples. The Resource Base will be the place where pupils collect adapted materials or the equipment they need to access the curriculum, and it may provide a quiet place where they can catch up on class work, receive extra help and relate to other youngsters who have a visual impairment.

Learning support assistants (LSAs)

A greater number of pupils are now being supported both in primary and secondary schools by LSAs. Where there is good practice, the LSAs will work under the supervision of a qualified teacher of the visually impaired but in some instances they may have to support children with little direct assistance. Opportunities for professional training for LSAs are limited so it is important that they are included in school based in-service training. Collaboration between teachers and LSAs is essential and they need to be involved in curriculum planning so that they can:

- advise on any area of potential difficulty;
- prepare and adapt materials well in advance of the lesson being taught;
- check out places to be visited for any particular hazards;
- arrange for assistive technology such as closed circuit television (CCTV) to be in the room if necessary.

Such discussions ensure that the responsibility for 'teaching' the pupils is not left to the LSA and that the pupil with visual impairment does not become 'dependent' upon one adult and isolated from the normal contact with their peers.

The willingness of individual teachers to understand the challenges facing children and young people with a visual impairment is a key factor in successfully meeting their needs. The following chapters provide some of the essential information teachers will require to develop this understanding so that children with a visual impairment can flourish and reach their full potential within a mainstream setting.

CHAPTER 2

Understanding the causes of visual impairment and the assessment of vision

Heather Mason

Introduction

Sarah, a Key Stage 2 pupil in her local school, is a popular and lively girl. As you enter the classroom she is easily identifiable; she has white hair, very pale skin and wears distinctive tinted glasses. When she takes off her glasses, you might notice that her eyes move quite quickly and involuntarily from side-to-side (a condition called **nystagmus**); the speed of this movement can increase when Sarah is tired or under any kind of pressure. Near to where she works with her friends is a work station consisting of a colour closed circuit TV (CCTV) to enable her to magnify text to her preferred size, a laptop computer and space to keep her hand-held magnifiers and other specialist equipment she may require. On her table is a raised bookstand for reading and writing at a comfortable working distance. Windows have venetian blinds to control the amount of direct sunlight entering the room as Sarah has **photophobia** – a painful intolerance to bright light and glare. She enjoys wearing her baseball cap in the playground but has to be careful not to stay out in the direct sunlight as her skin burns very quickly.

Causes of visual impairment

Sarah has inherited a type of **albinism** and her visual impairment was quickly identified at birth. Not all children and young people are so easily identifiable as Sarah. Sometimes children with a visual impairment may go unnoticed as they may not even wear glasses! Many eye conditions (such as albinism) are hereditary and can be passed to the child through either one or both parents carrying the gene. Parents may not be aware of this, so the birth of their child with a visual impairment may have been a major shock. Other visual conditions may arise during the development of the foetus, for example as a result of viral infections such as rubella. During birth, trauma can occur, and for very small premature babies, **retinopathy of prematurity** can develop – a severe visual impairment. During their early years, a small number of children develop brain tumours and infections that cause a visual loss, and are at risk from road and other types of accidents. Some drug treatments administered for other conditions may also affect eyesight.

Classification of visual impairment

Visual impairments can be classified in many different ways but teachers need to understand the educational implications for the child. The child may experience:

- problems reading the notes from the blackboard or scanning information quickly;
- distortion of depth perception, colour perception, what is being seen and perceived;
- problems in maintaining and changing focus at near and far distances;
- visual discomfort and fatigue;

and consequently may require additional time to process the visual information.

It is difficult to generalise about the implications of a visual impairment as two pupils with similar visual condition and recorded visual acuity levels may have totally different needs. The way vision is used may be influenced by:

- the age of onset of the eye condition;
- the amount of early support by a specialist teacher of the visually impaired or teacher expectations;
- parental and family attitude;
- motivation, personality factors and the social and emotional security of the child;
- past experiences – negative and positive.

Types of visual impairment

Space does not allow for an in-depth look at all the individual eye conditions – 'easy-to-read' information can be found in the recommended reading at the end of the book. What is important is knowing the name of the condition and being able to find out as much as possible about the implications for accessing the different parts of the curriculum. For example, if a pupil has severe **myopia** (shortsightedness), the wearing of their spectacles or contact lenses will be crucial for them.[1] Without their spectacles, such pupils will be unable

---

[1] Many pupils take off their spectacles for reading and hold the work very close to their eye to take advantage of natural magnification

to follow any teacher demonstration or see objects clearly within a few feet of them. Of course, many pupils have to be encouraged to wear their spectacles as they are victims of peer pressure and in some instances teasing or even bullying. Usually, conditions such as **albinism** and **myopia** are fairly stable but others such as **retinitis pigmentosa**, a disease that affects the retina causing tunnel vision and night blindness, can be progressive. Knowing this can alert the teacher to be observant about any changes in behaviour and academic progress and to take appropriate action. Similarly, such knowledge can help in planning an appropriate working environment, adaptation of worksheets and teaching strategies in advance of any lesson.

Figure 2.1 lists the most common eye conditions and summarises some of the implications of them. It is a general guide as there are always exceptions to the rule. Some pupils may have more than one condition. Further information about individuals will be available from the specialist teacher of the visually impaired and, of course, the pupils themselves should always be involved in any decision making about their learning. An annotated diagram of the eye is provided on page 60.

Assessing vision

The Statement of Special Educational Needs will usually include information from visual assessments, including measurements of visual acuity (the sharpness and clarity of vision) and information on how the child uses vision on a day-to-day basis – their functional vision. Visual acuity tests will normally provide information regarding the child's distance and near vision, field of vision, colour perception, ability to discern contrast and other relevant information, for instance, whether any low vision aids (e.g. magnifiers) have been recommended, suggestions for lighting levels or advice on any physical restrictions such as participation in contact sports. The field of vision represents the total area the child can see when looking straight ahead and the most severely reduced visual fields may result in 'tunnel vision'. While loss of colour perception occurs in the red/green part of the spectrum in about 8 per cent of all boys with normal vision, a rarer type of loss may also include blue/yellow deficiency. Problems will occur when activities require a high level of colour discrimination. Issues relating to distance and near visual acuity deserve further explanation.

Distance vision

All teachers are familiar with the 'Snellen eye test' – a chart made up of lines of letters of diminishing sizes. The line of letters or other symbols are carefully

condition	increased lighting	decreased lighting	intolerance to glare	good contrast needed	enlarged print	benefits from LVAs
albinism	no	yes	yes	yes	yes	yes
aniridia	no	yes	yes	yes	yes	yes
aphakia	yes	no	yes	yes	yes	yes
astigmatism	no	no	yes	yes	yes	yes
buphthalmus	no	yes	yes	yes	yes	yes
cataract–central	no	yes	yes	yes	no	no
cataract–peripheral	yes	no	yes	yes	yes	yes
coloboma	no	yes	yes	yes	yes	yes
cone dystrophy	no	yes	yes	yes	yes	yes
glaucoma	yes	no	yes	yes	yes	yes
hypermetropia	no	no	yes	yes	yes	yes
keratoconus	no	no	yes	yes	yes	yes
macular problems	yes	no	yes	yes	yes	yes
myopia	yes	no	no	yes	yes	yes
nystagmus	no	no	yes	yes	yes	yes
optic atrophy and hypoplasia	yes	no	no	yes	yes	yes
photophobia	no	yes	yes	yes	no	no
retinitis pigmentosa	no	yes	yes	yes	no	CCTV
squint	yes	no	yes	yes	yes	no
uveitis	yes	no	yes	yes	yes	yes

Figure 2.1   Educational implications of common visual eye conditions

calculated so they can be recognised at a certain distance by a person with normal vision, e.g. 60m, 36m, 24m, 18m, 12m, 9m, 6m and 5m.

Measurements of distance visual acuity reflects how far a child sits from the chart and the lowest line that the child can read. For example, if at 6m from the chart, only the top single letter can be read, then the measurement of visual acuity is 6/60 or to put it another way, the child can only see at 6m what a fully sighted child could see at 60m. If children cannot read even the top letter at 6m, they would be asked to go closer to the chart until they identify it. A visual acuity of 3/60 means that the child can read the top letter at 3 metres and 1/36 indicates that the second line of the chart was read at 1 metre. Obviously, for

Figure 2.2   A Snellen Eye Chart (not to scale)

children with a severe visual impairment, other clinical tests in addition to this one will be used to determine their acuity. Although this is useful information, it does not indicate how well vision is used. This is illustrated clearly by the true case histories of two pupils.

James and Karl, aged 11, had congenital **cataracts** and visual acuities of 6/60. James, the eldest of four children, was highly motivated to use his vision for school work, enjoying a range of physical activities such as football and swimming. He moved quite independently around the school and his neighbourhood, helping his mother with shopping and tasks within the home. At school, he was very popular and it was difficult to believe on many occasions that he had a severe visual impairment. Karl, who had an older sister, was reluctant to read and write print or to use the CCTV that had been bought specifically for him. He shunned any physical activities and constantly brought notes to school to excuse him from swimming. Karl's table manners were very poor, and he persisted in eating with his fingers. After PE, he had great difficulties in buttoning his shirt and tying shoelaces! Weekends were spent in bed listening to pop music and being fed finger food. Karl, an intelligent boy, was functioning as a much younger 'blind' child in many respects – he wasn't motivated to make the best use of his vision.

Near vision

Near vision acuity is used for tasks such as reading, writing and other types of close work. Testing of near vision usually consists of reading print of different sizes measured in 'N' – the higher the N number, the larger the print. This is very important information as it is a guide to the size of print the pupil can read in optimum lighting conditions without using a low vision aid (LVA), such as a hand-held magnifier. It is worth talking to your pupils about their preferred typeface and font size. Some fonts such as Arial and Helvetica have been found to be easier to read than others by young people with low vision.

Functional vision

For pupils such as Karl, Sarah and James to be successful in school, a full assessment of their individual needs is essential. A thorough assessment can inform decisions about adaptations to the working environment, teaching and learning methods, the additional skills the child needs to learn (e.g. mobility and orientation) and what is required in terms of technology to give full access to the curriculum.

Alongside the information from the clinical tests, the teacher will want to know how the child uses their vision in and outside of the classroom in academic, non-academic and social activities. Children's ability to use their vision efficiently will depend on many factors, for instance the personality of the child (as shown in the examples of Karl and James), environmental conditions and the sensitivity in which activities have been adapted take into account the visual difficulties experienced by the pupil. We know from our own experiences that there are occasions when we want to use our vision more keenly. The teacher of the visually impaired would normally carry out a functional visual assessment and highlight areas needing urgent attention – these recommendations might form part of the IEP. For example, visual perceptual skills of younger children such as the ability to scan, track, discriminate, recognise patterns and symmetry, hand–eye coordination skills are normally assessed by the teacher of the visually impaired and a range of activities to develop these can be built into the curriculum. It is important that every opportunity is taken to encourage a child with a visual impairment to use

36

ann is six.

24

ann is six.   ann has a bun in a bag.   spot is not a big dog. he is just a pup.

18

spot sits up and begs.   ann gives him a bit of her bun.   ann is not as big as tom. tom is seven.   tom can hop skip and run.   he has a sand pit in his garden. spot ann and tom romp and jump in the sand.   spot barks.

12

last winter we had a robin nest in the hedge.   we fed it on crusts.   dip the crusts in milk.

10

dad has ten fat hens in a hut at the bottom of the garden.   he fed corn to his hens from a pan in his hand.

8

let us run and tell dad his hens have laid.   perhaps he will have an egg for supper.

6

on a sunny summer day it is fun to sit under a tree and listen to a lark singing in the sky.   a farmer sits on a tractor carting hay.   let us ask him if we may ride on the hay to the farm.   is it scones and jam for tea?   if we run home after the ride we will not be late.

Figure 2.3   Example of N print test (not to scale)

Name:

Date of birth   **Age**

Visual impairment/s

Additional impairments

Date of last (i) clinical assessment   **(ii) functional assessment**

Visual acuity

uncorrected	Distance L	Distance R	Binocular
corrected	Distance L	Distance R	Binocular
	Near L	Near R	Binocular

Can read   N print at   cm

Field of vision			normal (Y/N)
		Central	Y/N
		Peripheral	Y/N
		hemianopia	Y/N
Colour perception	Y/N		
Light sensitivity			Y/N
Ability to see in the dark			Y/N
Contrast sensitivity			Y/N
Ability to discern moving objects			Y/N

LVA prescription

	Near	Distance
	CCTV	

Visual functioning with LVAs

Can read size	N print at	cm
Estimation of speed of reading for near distance is		wpm
Estimation of distance at which objects can be discerned		m

Appropriate lighting levels

Restrictions on physical activity

Medication

Additional comments, e.g. summary of any functional vision test

Figure 2.4   Example of a summary of clinical and functional information

their vision and not to rely upon a friend or an adult when a task may be visually demanding. It is helpful if a summary of the clinical and functional vision information is kept by all class and subject teachers and learning support assistants.

Low vision aids or devices (LVA/Ds)

Many pupils with low vision benefit from using a low vision aid. Examples of these (see Figure 2.5) may include spectacles, hand-held telescopes, binoculars, stand or hand-held magnifiers, illuminated magnifiers, and closed circuit TV magnifiers (CCTV). LVAs, apart from CCTVs, are usually prescribed free of charge after the child has seen an optometrist attached to a Low Vision Clinic. Prescription follows a full clinical assessment which takes into account the educational and leisure needs of the pupil. A CCTV is usually provided from the normal school/LEA finances, and should be available to those children who will benefit from using one.

When an LVA/D has been prescribed, the child must undergo specific training in its efficient use. This is usually the responsibility of the advisory teacher in the

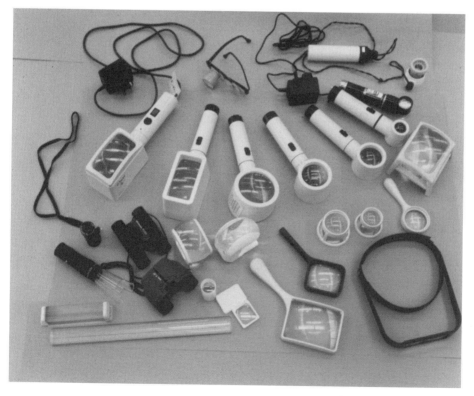

Figure 2.5   Examples of Low vision aids

first instance, as the use of it may involve developing a new set of complex skills. From a very early age, children can be taught to be responsible for the care and maintenance of their own LVA/Ds (including spectacles), although it is useful if an adult is responsible for carrying out a weekly check on their use, perhaps as part of a check of the child's specialist equipment. Obviously, once prescribed, the pupil needs to be given time to adjust to a new way of working – increased use leads to greater independence. Reluctant users, especially those who have been teased by other children or who lack motivation, need sensitive handling by the teacher.

The strength of the lens of the LVA/D is expressed in dioptres. By dividing this number by 4 the magnification can be calculated. For example, a 10 dioptre hand–held magnifier would enlarge the print approximately 2.5 times. The higher the magnification, the smaller the field of view and the amount of information which can be processed. This has implications for the speed at which the child can work. The high magnification used by pupils with severe visual difficulties often results in visual fatigue with prolonged usage (you may like to try using one of the LVAs for a short period of time to experience the difficulties of use).

CCTVs electronically enlarge printed material onto a TV screen and are used by those pupils with severe visual impairments. They can enlarge text up to 64x but at this level of magnification only one or two letters can be viewed on the screen at a time. They have useful facilities such as allowing children to read one line or even one word at a time, to reverse polarity to white print on a black background and to vary levels of contrast and illumination. Colour CCTVs, although expensive, are a boon for map work and demonstrations. CCTVs can be a valuable resource in the primary school but are especially useful in secondary schools; however they are often underused, usually because they are placed in an area where there is not easy access at all times of the day, for example in the geography room. As many are not easily portable, forward planning is necessary to make sure that the CCTV is available in the right place at the right time.

Recommended reading

Mason, H. L. (1992) 'Visual impairments', in Gulliford, R. and Upton, G. (eds) *Special Educational Needs*, 111–127. London: Routledge.

Mason, H. L. and Lomas, J. (1992) 'Visual impairment in the mainstream'. *Special.* 1(1) 41–44.

Mason, H. L. (1995) *Spotlight on Special Educational Needs*. Tamworth: NASEN publications.

Mason, H. L., McCall, S. *et al.* (1997) *Visual Impairment: Access to Education for Children and Young People*. London: David Fulton Publishers.

Useful web sites

Lea Hyvarinen's resource pages: http: //med-aapos.bu.edu/leaweb/index.html
Royal National Institute for the Blind: http: //www.rnib.org.uk/
Scottish Sensory Service: http: //www.ssc.mhie.ac.uk/

CHAPTER 3

Environmental issues

Christine Arter

Introduction

When thinking about the school environment for pupils with a visual impairment, safety issues are of paramount importance. There has long been a debate about the importance of adapting the school environment, not only to make it safe for pupils with a visual impairment, but to make access easier. While no one will disagree about those measures taken to make the environment a safe and secure place for all pupils, some would argue that school is preparing pupils to take an independent role in the wider society that makes few adaptations for those with disabilities. They would suggest that limited adaptations should be made to the school environment and that pupils with a visual impairment should learn how to function independently and safely within the school and the wider environment.

Whatever the view taken, a careful audit of the school environment by a fully qualified teacher of the visually impaired is recommended, to establish where simple improvements may be made, and where dangers exist, so that steps may be taken to minimise or eliminate these. If pupils with a visual impairment feel confident in a safe school environment, then their assurance in finding their way around the classroom and the school campus will grow. Pupils who are visually impaired may need guidance from a qualified teacher of the visually impaired or a mobility instructor to enable them to move around the school with safety.

Major adaptation of the school environment would be required to meet all the needs of the child with a visual impairment, and the costs involved would be huge. However, there is much that can be done by adopting some simple techniques in the classroom and across the school as a whole. Often economics dictate that choices must be made and desired changes will often need to be prioritised.

In the classroom

Seating position

It is essential for teachers to ensure that they understand the full implications of the pupil's eye condition. It may be that for the child with low vision, their sight is better in one eye than the other. Ensure that the child sits at the front, on the side of the room that allows the pupil the optimum opportunity to see the teacher, the blackboard, the TV or practical demonstrations. Remember that the child who has little or no sight in their right eye will need to sit facing the front, slightly to the right of centre, to enable them to use their left eye to maximum effect.

Many pupils with a visual impairment will find the glare caused by sunlight shining through windows to be a problem. Some eye conditions, for example cataracts, may mean that the child needs increased levels of light; however this needs to be carefully controlled and directed, and the glare caused by sunlight is often unhelpful. For other pupils, such as those with albinism for example, too much light may cause real discomfort resulting in a considerable decrease in their ability to see anything clearly. It is important therefore that these factors be taken into account when choosing the child's optimum seating position. Always ask the child what is most comfortable and be guided by them. As a general rule, it is usually safe to assume that blinds or thick curtains will be required, to control lighting levels within the classroom where a child with a visual impairment is working. Even when blinds or curtains are available they may be defective; a careful check should be made to ensure that they are working effectively.

It is important for the teacher to remember to stand away from the window (the major source of light) as the glare may prevent the child from looking at, or seeing, the teacher.

> Joe is a boy of 11 years of age. He has **optic atrophy** and his sight is slowly deteriorating. No glasses have been prescribed. His optimum working position seems to be at the side of the room, where there is a plug to enable him to use an individual task light, with the light source aimed directly onto his work. The position of the plug (and the fixed storage units) mean that Joe's desk is very close to the window. Glare from the window on most days makes it impossible for Joe to see his work. Even with the vertical blinds drawn, the light from outside causes him problems. The difficulty has been overcome by firmly fixing black sugar paper to the windows by Joe's desk, to eliminate glare. Joe is unable to see work presented on the blackboard and needs the information displayed on a separate sheet.

Copying from the board may be a problem for the pupil with a visual impairment. If a blackboard or whiteboard is used, the writing should be clear and the board should be regularly cleaned. A clean whiteboard or blackboard will result in a clearer contrast between the background and the writing. It may be preferable to provide the pupil with a separate written summary sheet. This does of course mean that advanced planning and preparation is required.

The importance of avoiding glare from windows has been emphasised; however it is important that the correct lighting levels are maintained. Good, ambient lighting is essential for pupils with a visual impairment. Situations where there are pools of bright light and then contrasting gloomy, dimly-lit areas should be avoided. The use of individual task lighting is helpful for some pupils, while other pupils prefer lower levels of light. The pupil should be involved in discussions about lighting levels and their views should be sought about what is best for them.

The child's working position

The child's eye condition may mean that in order to see clearly they need to adopt an unusual working position. This is called *eccentric viewing*. The child with **nystagmus** for example, may have considerable difficulty in fixation and may turn their head to one side to find the eye position in which the movement of their eyes is most effectively reduced. Eccentric viewing should not be discouraged. Pupils may also need to peer very closely at their work in order to be able to actually see it. The adoption of such unusual working positions may result in fatigue. It is important therefore to make sure that pupils with a visual impairment are provided with the appropriate furniture. Desks and chairs should be at an optimum height to allow the pupil to sit comfortably. It may be advantageous to provide the pupil with a desk that has an adjustable top, that allows the work surface to be raised, thus avoiding the situation where the pupil is stooping down to their work for prolonged periods. Pupils do not always choose to raise the desk top, even when the facility is provided for them; many pupils try very hard to avoid being different to their peers. This is true for pupils of all ages but is especially important to adolescents. Sometimes book stands or adjustable magnet boards may be used to raise work to a more appropriate height for pupils with low vision. Again, use of these may be avoided by pupils not wishing to appear different.

The size of the desk is another important consideration. Sometimes pupils may need their work enlarging to A3 size, although it must be remembered that merely enlarging work is not always the ideal solution. Enlarged papers are often cumbersome and difficult to use, and pupils will need to use a desk that allows sufficient space to work with comfort. They will also need space to store their papers in folders of an appropriate size. The child who uses Braille will need a desk that is suitably large to hold their brailler and large, bulky Braille books, and they will also need space to store the large folders that are used to house

Figure 3.1   Using an adjustable book stand

their brailled work. Pupils should be involved in discussions about how best to store their work and how they can readily retrieve completed work.

Pupils with a visual impairment often need to use a range of equipment to help them access the curriculum. They may need to use a tape recorder, a CCTV, a task light or laptop computer to type their work. Electric sockets are often situated to the side of the room, and may result in a situation where the pupil with a visual impairment works in an isolated position, away from their peers. This is not an easy situation to overcome and has implications for the child's ability to socialise with their peers. Extension leads clearly present a hazard and are not a solution to the problem. It is essential therefore that the teacher organises the class in such a way that they ensure that the pupil with a visual impairment is included, perhaps in group work for example. In all situations the teacher should try to avoid isolating the pupil or making them appear different.

Storage of materials

Careful and consistent classroom organisation should be adopted and maintained to assist the pupil with visual impairment and to help them achieve

Figure 3.2 Using a closed circuit television (CCTV)

greater independence. At the beginning of the school year the classroom layout and the storage of materials should be explained to all pupils. Pupils should be informed of any changes made. All pupils, including those with a visual impairment, should be encouraged to collect their own materials and then put them away carefully at the end of the lesson. Books and storage boxes, etc. should be clearly labelled in either large print or Braille as appropriate.

Ensure that the class understand the pupil's eye condition and encourage them to get into the habit of pushing chairs in as they stand and keeping bags, coats and other belongings safely stowed out of the way.

Display of work

Work should be displayed at a suitable height to enable the pupil to see it. This is a simple and obvious statement but it may be difficult to achieve, since in many schools notice boards in both classrooms and corridors are often placed too high for pupils with a visual impairment to see them easily. The implications for display of work for pupils with low vision who use print, and those who are blind and use Braille, are clearly different. For the Braille user, labels and tactile displays need to be at hand height, while print displays for the child with low vision need to be at eye level. For the child with low vision, work displays should be mounted on a clearly contrasting background, and clear, large print should be used. For example, white paper can be mounted on a black background and then mounted on a bright background to highlight it. Luminous colours are often used to good effect, and although the extra work is time-consuming and possibly tedious, the extra effort will result in an effective display which will be attractive to all.

Wall displays are sometimes laminated with a shiny plastic material to preserve them. The reasoning behind this measure is clear, but the glare of reflected light on the shiny surface will make them inaccessible for many pupils with a visual impairment.

The wider school environment

School corridors, stairways and dining halls are notoriously difficult places for pupils and staff to find their way among jostling crowds of pupils. Careful consideration should be given to the wider school environment to enable the pupil with a visual impairment to find their way safely around the school, thus further encouraging independence and avoiding the situation where the child appears 'different'.

Many of the important whole-school issues concerning the school environment may be those over which class teachers, particularly newly qualified teachers, have little control. All teachers have an important role as advocates of pupils with a visual impairment; they may for example make suggestions to the SENCO or members of the senior management team about improvements that may be made when new furniture or floorings are purchased, or when the school is redecorated. Some of the more important considerations will now be discussed.

Decor

Clear print, Braille or tactile labels should be provided as signposts for pupils with a visual impairment. The painting of doors, skirting boards and door surrounds in bold, contrasting colours is often very useful for pupils with low vision. A contrasting skirting board may be used as a guide by pupils with low vision, as they find their way around the school building. Sometimes a contrasting line may be painted on the floor as a guiding line. Door furniture and electric light switches which provide a good, clear, colour contrast are sometimes used to great advantage. A cheap means of providing contrast may be achieved by using brightly coloured adhesive tape around a light switch for example. Care must be taken to ensure that the tape is maintained and is not allowed to become worn and therefore ineffective.

When schools are repainted some consideration should be given to the paint used, not only to provide contrast, but to avoid large wall areas causing problems with glare as the shiny surface reflects light.

Furniture

When expensive items such as furniture and floor coverings are to be replaced, the needs of the pupil with a visual impairment should be taken into account. Furniture that provides a clear colour contrast from surrounding floor or wall areas is much easier for the pupil with low vision to see. Table tops or work surfaces are often made of shiny material that causes uncomfortable glare for many pupils with a visual impairment. This is an important consideration when buying new furniture. Some teachers overcome the problems of glare from working surfaces, by covering them with matt sugar paper or a non-shiny tray that provides a good colour contrast to the work materials being used. Neither approach is entirely satisfactory since neither means provides a permanent solution to the problem; however these approaches can be used to good effect from time to time.

Floor coverings

Floor surfaces also need careful consideration. For the pupil with a visual impairment, different floor coverings often provide an extremely useful clue when finding their way around the wider school environment. For example, mats placed by doors leading to or from the playground, allowing pupils to wipe their feet as they enter the school, provide a useful landmark to pupils with a visual impairment. Similarly, carpeted areas in classrooms may be used by pupils to orientate themselves within the room. It is an important consideration that carpeted areas within the classroom often provide an effective means of keeping the noise down in a busy classroom. This is important for pupils with a visual impairment who depend more heavily on their listening skills for learning and as a means of orientating themselves within the room. Listening enables the pupil with a visual impairment to find out what other pupils in the class are doing. Pupils with a visual impairment may use more taped materials than their peers who are fully sighted, and again a noisy environment may make it more difficult to concentrate and listen.

It is important to remember that both bright sunlight and artificial lighting shining on to highly polished floors may be another source of uncomfortable glare, and teachers need to be vigilant to ensure that floor coverings, such as floor tiles or carpeting, do not become broken or curled at the edges, and thus present a danger to the pupil with impaired vision.

David is blind, with some perception of light. He always knows where he is in the school environment and he may be seen confidently walking around his primary school. David uses many environmental clues to help him. He knows for example that there are mats by the playground and the front entrance doors. On bright, sunny days, he uses the light coming in from the windows on the front corridor to orientate himself.

The cloakroom area

Cloakroom areas are frequently difficult areas for pupils with a visual impairment. The lighting is often poor and coats and other belongings are usually found strewn across the floor, causing a hazard. It is difficult to manage such areas of the school to ensure that they are kept clear and safe for the pupil with a visual impairment. Improved lighting could be installed and pupils should be encouraged to keep the area tidy and the floor clear. In primary schools perhaps it would be possible to provide the pupil with a visual impairment with a coat peg that is easily located next to the classroom door.

In corridors, cloakrooms and classrooms teachers should be aware of the positioning of heaters and/or radiators, which may be very hot during winter months. It may be necessary for such potential hazards to be guarded or moved. Fire extinguishers are sometimes situated in such a position as to cause potential harm, and the positioning of these should be carefully considered.

Staircases

Stairs are often another problem area for pupils with a visual impairment. The difficulties encountered by pupils with sun streaming through windows, causing glare, has already been discussed. Sunlight flooding in on to staircases is a common hazard. Equally, problems may occur when staircases are dimly lit. In large schools the number of pupils using staircases at the change of lessons often cause problems for fully sighted pupils and staff alike! They may be very frightening for pupils with a visual impairment.

Measures may be taken to help to minimise the problems for pupils with a visual impairment. Where lighting is poor, additional glare-free lighting should be installed and a school rule encouraging pupils to move along one side of corridors and staircases often proves to be effective. Sometimes it is desirable and possible to paint the nosings of stairs in a bright, contrasting colour. Bright yellow appears to be the most commonly used colour for this purpose. For the child who is blind, textured edges to stairs would provide a useful cue. These measures would also prove useful on any steps outside the school building. A brightly coloured banister may also be a useful guide for a pupil with low vision.

Sometimes buildings are designed in such a way that the edge of a staircase presents a hazard to pupils standing by, or moving underneath, the staircase. In such a case the hazard should be clearly and boldly marked for the pupil with a visual impairment. For the blind child a different floor texture might be used to warn of the danger. In other buildings there are posts or pillars which are placed in prominent positions, both within the school building and outside. These should be similarly marked.

Glass doors present a danger to all pupils but are especially hazardous to those with low vision. It might be possible to mark the doors effectively to lessen the danger. Self-closing mechanisms may be installed on doors, or they may be firmly fixed in an open position. Advice should be sought from the school Safety Officer about fire doors.

Whenever measures are taken to highlight areas of danger it is essential that the quality of the markings be maintained. It is a common problem in schools, that care has been taken initially to mark potential hazards, but over time the markings are allowed to fade and disappear. Frayed tape at the edge of steps is likely to become another potential danger.

The outside environment

Pathways

Outdoor pathways are often a cause for concern within the school environment. If they have a clear, raised edge they may be used advantageously by the pupil with a visual impairment as an under-foot guide. All too often however, the edges of paths become worn or broken and become an additional hazard which may trip the child. Textured paving may be used to good effect; however, uneven paving slabs or paths may cause pupils to trip or fall and injure themselves. Sometimes pupils use such inconsistencies as a landmark to help them find their way about the wider school environment. For example, pupils may learn that they turn to the left or right at the point where the raised edge is broken, or where the paving slab rocks.

Bushes or trees are often allowed to grow across pathways. These may at best prevent the child from using the edge of the path as a means of trailing, and at worst may present a danger to the pupil, causing them to scratch or hurt themselves on the branches. Scented shrubs or bushes may be used to provide a clue, to enable pupils with a visual impairment to orientate themselves and find their way around the school campus.

Sometimes, where a pathway is situated close to the school building, the situation arises where doors or windows open outwards on to the path. If these doors or windows are left open they may present a hazard to the pupil with a visual impairment. Solutions to such problems are not always easy. The pupil with a visual impairment might be advised not to use a particular route around the school, but it is possible that the pathway is the only safe route for the pupil. It is suggested that in such situations each hazard be carefully studied and a safe procedure be adopted to suit the particular circumstances. Advice should be sought from a mobility instructor or a qualified teacher of the visually impaired.

Steps

Steps outside in the school grounds may present a problem to pupils with a visual impairment. They should be clearly marked to help pupils find their way around independently. Handrails may need to be provided, especially if, for example, there is a drop down to one side of the steps.

The playground

Sometimes seats are provided for pupils in the playground. These might be placed in isolation or near a pathway and may present a hazard to the pupil with a visual impairment. With training it may be possible for the pupil to create a mental map or picture of where such features are situated and thus avoid the danger of bumping into them unexpectedly.

It is important to consider whether there are shaded areas where the pupil with **photophobia**, for example, can sit or stand in comfort on bright days. Furthermore, it might be advisable to provide a quiet area where pupils with limited or no useful vision can safely avoid rowdy games or footballs.

Conclusion

It is vital that pupils with a visual impairment are not over-protected, but at the same time their needs and safety should be given due consideration. Some adaptations and measures may be taken to easily solve potential problems, others will take longer to remedy and may incur considerable costs. This chapter is not intended to provide all of the answers to problems associated with the school environment, but it is hoped that it will enable the teacher who is new to the field of visual impairment to look at their teaching situation both critically and with some understanding, enabling them to provide a safer environment for pupils with a visual impairment.

Recommended reading

Best, A. B. (1992) *Teaching Children with Visual Impairments.* Milton Keynes: Open University Press.

Chapman, E. K. and Stone, J. M. (1988) *The Visually Handicapped Child in Your Classroom.* London: Cassell.

Lomas, J. and Ackerley, B. (1995) 'An environmental audit' *Eye Contact* Number 12, Summer 1995 supplement.

Mason, H., McCall, S. *et al.* (1997) Visual Impairment: *Access to Education for Children and Young People.* Chapter 21. London: David Fulton Publishers.

CHAPTER 4

Accessing the curriculum

Steve McCall

In the previous chapter the issues relating to the general learning environment for the children with a visual impairment were considered. In this chapter we shall explore how children with a visual impairment can best be given access to learning materials and how they can be encouraged to develop their communication skills through reading and writing.

Print

All children in the class will benefit from the provision of clear reading materials. The guidelines for presenting materials to children with a visual impairment are useful when selecting textbooks, reading books or when preparing worksheets for any child.

At one time it was widely believed that all reading materials for children with a visual impairment needed to be in large type. We now know that, with the appropriate LVAs and training, even children with very low vision can use standard print sizes for some purposes. However in many cases enlarging the print can help make close work less tiring. The preferred print size will vary according to the degree of the child's residual vision, the nature of the task and the complexity of the text. An advisory teacher should be able to give guidance about the requirements of the individual child. The legibility of print depends not only on its size but on its quality. Factors such as the typeface, the spacing between letters, words and lines, the quality of the paper, the layout of the page, the density of the ink and its contrast with the paper all have an effect on how comfortable and user-friendly reading materials are for the child with a visual impairment.

When assessing the suitability of a textbook for a child with low vision, both the print and the layout of the book need consideration. Clearly, books in which the spacing between the lines is cramped and the margins are narrow are likely to be uncomfortable for any child to read, but there are some particular considerations for children with a visual impairment which are not quite so obvious. For example, textbooks which rely heavily on illustrations (such as those used in modern language lessons) need particular thought. Unless the photographs or drawings are close to the relevant text, the child may need to spend considerable time and effort scanning the page to make sense of the exercise.

For most children, black print on white paper provides the best contrast, but the paper should have a matt finish to avoid glare. Text which strays over illustrations can be particularly difficult to read, especially if the illustrations are in colour. Print which is in colour may prove difficult to read unless it contrasts well with the background. Complex graphs or tables in textbooks will often require modification for the child with low vision. They may need to be redesigned in a simplified form using a word processor, or photocopied, enlarged and then simplified. In many books, adaptation of at least part of the text will be necessary for some children, but carefully chosen textbooks can minimise the number of changes required.

The preparation of worksheets suitable for children with low vision is now a relatively straightforward process for teachers with access to word processing facilities. Word processors allow teachers to control the typeface, font size, layout and spacing between the lines. Where teachers have access to ink jet printers or laser printers, they can provide materials of excellent quality which can be adapted for a child's individual preferences. In schools where there is a Resource Base for children with a visual impairment a copy of the material on disk can be provided in advance for the specialist teacher to adapt.

There is no single typeface that is recommended for children with a visual impairment but fonts such as Helvetica or Arial present a bold and clean typeface that most children with low vision prefer. The preferred size of print will vary from child to child. Many children with low vision use materials printed in font sizes within the 18 to 24 point range, printed in bold with ×1½ or × 2 spacing between the lines, but the Advisory Teacher should be able to offer help in choosing the best parameters for the individual child.

For some children with low vision, enlarging print may actually work to their disadvantage. For example children with a severe field loss, as often occurs in conditions such as **retinitis pigmentosa**, may have a small working area of vision, and enlarging print means that they can actually see less at each fixation. Nevertheless many children with low vision will find it easier to work from enlarged print in some situations.

Most school photocopiers have facilities for enlarging learning materials, but thought needs to be given to the guidance from the LEA on the laws of copyright. The Copyright Licensing Agency (CLA) have concluded an agreement with the RNIB which allows enlarged photocopies (minimum 16 point) to be

18 Point Helvetica Bold

18 Point Arial Bold

24 Point Helvetica Bold

24 Point Arial Bold

Figure 4.1   Examples of print type faces

made for use by children with low vision for the purposes of instruction, but electronic storage of material is not permitted under this agreement. In the case of any doubt, it is advisable to consult the Schools Licensing Officer at the RNIB.

Factors which will affect legibility of enlarged materials include the quality of the original print and the presence of background colours. It may be necessary to use the 'darken' control to improve the print contrast. Enlargement from A4 to A3 paper brings with it problems for the child of manageability of large sheets. Scanning the original material into a computer and then increasing the font size and adjusting the layout enables enlarged material to be produced on A4 paper.

Some eye conditions affect children's ability to focus (or accommodate). Children with severe **hypermetropia** (long-sightedness) may find it very difficult to sustain very close work such as reading for more than a few minutes. Conditions such as **nystagmus** affect children's ability to control their eye movements and they may find it difficult to keep their place on a line when reading or interpreting tables. A loss in the central visual field can make it difficult for children to locate information on a diagram. A severe field loss, which may reduce the number of letters a child can see at a single glance, will make activities such as skimming a text much more difficult. The degree to which children are sensitive to light is another factor which may have an important bearing on their performance in the classroom; for example children may find it extremely uncomfortable to look at a teacher who stands near a bright window when talking to the class.

The specialist teacher should be able to provide the class teacher with information about the implications of the child's eye condition for both close work and reading from the workboard. Some children will be able to read work presented on the workboard but the child with a visual impairment will need particular consideration when a video or overhead projector is used. The child will need to be appropriately positioned and the teacher may need to provide additional commentary to ensure the meaning is clear.

The provision of appropriately adapted reading and study materials can help children with a visual impairment to study with greater accuracy for longer periods but it can also help make learning easier for all children in the class.

Handwriting

There are wide variations in the handwriting of children with a visual impairment. Some do learn to write neatly and legibly but others find the acquisition of handwriting skills a tedious and frustrating process and they find the goals in the National Curriculum of legibility and fluency in handwriting difficult to achieve.

> Grant is in Year 4. He has a distance visual acuity of 6/60 as a result of **optic atrophy**. Although he sits at the front of the class he cannot read from the board. He uses print for all his work, and his English SATs (Standard Attainment Tests) suggest his reading is above average. He is writing up a final version of a story he drafted out yesterday. He is using a sloping writing stand illuminated by a fluorescent anglepoise lamp. A simple line marker made from coloured card helps him to keep his place while he copies from the draft version. He writes with a black felt-tip pen, on wide-lined paper. He works steadily but needs extra time to complete his story. His handwriting in the draft version started off neatly but became more and more untidy and he now finds it hard to read back the last part of what he has written. The LSA asks him if the closed circuit television magnifier will help. He doesn't think so; he can see the work but can't interpret his writing. The LSA suggests that the new typing lessons will help him, and that by the end of the year he will be able to write all his stories on a computer.

There are a number of reasons why children with a visual impairment can experience difficulties in developing neat handwriting. Vision plays a major part in helping children to refine the fine motor skills and spatial concepts that neat writing requires, and children with a visual impairment may have had fewer opportunities than their classmates to develop their motor skills through play before they started school. Low vision can restrict the chances for refining movements by observing and imitating the actions of others. As a result, some children will find pen control difficult to achieve and their writing may be excessively large, uneven and their letter formation may be inconsistent. The visual factors noted in the previous section which affect reading will make it harder for the child to copy. The constant relocation and focusing of the gaze that copying requires can be time-consuming and fatiguing. Children with low vision may find it particularly difficult to follow the teacher's demonstrations to the class of how letter shapes are formed.

Some children will need to work very close to the page in order to see what they are writing. Their cramped working position will make fatigue more likely and will make it harder for the teacher to ensure that the correct level of lighting is reaching the page or to monitor the quality of the work as the child is writing. These difficulties are likely to be exacerbated if the child is left-handed or has vision in only one eye. The use of a sloping desktop workstand and appropriate task lighting can be of great help to some children.

For children with a visual impairment, writing in a straight line with even spacing between words can be particularly challenging. Especially in the early stages, the use of lined paper can be helpful in establishing how the ascenders and descenders of a letter should be positioned. Lined paper especially produced for children with low vision is available through your specialist teacher. The writing implement the child uses also needs careful consideration. Fountain pens often provide the best contrast but they are difficult for younger children to maintain. Black fibre-tipped handwriting pens, such as those produced by Berol, are an excellent compromise for children of all ages provided they are regularly checked for wear. If the child is using a pencil, then HB pencils should be avoided because they produce a poor contrast. Some children find that triangular pen grips can greatly improve their pen control.

There is a difference of opinion about the handwriting style that should be taught to children with a visual impairment. Although some specialists advocate that cursive script should be taught from the start, most children with a visual impairment in the UK begin with print and move to cursive writing once print writing has been established. Whatever method is chosen the child is likely to need individual support to establish the correct sequences of letter formation.

Handwriting is an essential skill both in school and in social life and children with a visual impairment should be encouraged to develop a clear legible style. Children with low vision may find that, as they progress in their schooling, the increasing demands of the curriculum will make handwriting an inefficient medium to record their work and they will need to develop typing skills in order to reach the standards of speed and neatness that the rest of their peers will achieve. Proficient touch-typing can enable a child to write quickly and legibly and access to word processing facilities can help overcome difficulties in spelling and grammar. Training in typing is often introduced to children with low vision at the ages of 8 or 9 and specialist typing tutor programmes have been developed for children with low vision. (These are available from the Research Centre for the Education of the Visually Handicapped at the School of Education, University of Birmingham. The full address is given at the end of this book.)

Spelling

There is evidence that children with a visual impairment are more likely to experience difficulties in achieving the levels of accuracy in spelling expected of their classmates. In general they will have had less exposure to the written word in the environment; for example they may be unable to see the advertising captions on hoardings, on the side of buses, on shelves in shops or on television.

The ability to recognise the pattern of a whole word at a glance is a crucial skill in recognising whether or not words are spelt correctly. Some children with a visual impairment may be unable to see the whole word at a glance. However, some of the techniques developed to improve the spelling of children who are fully sighted can be successfully adapted for children with a visual impairment. For example, the technique of 'look, cover and write' has been successfully used with children with a range of visual impairments. (For a full discussion of the use of this technique with pupils with a visual impairment, see Arter and Mason 1994.)

Listening

As children progress through the National Curriculum, the amount and complexity of information they have to deal with steadily increases. Much of the information in the mainstream classroom is presented visually, either through the written word or through diagrams and tables, photographs, drawings and television and video. In some circumstances children with a visual impairment may find that hearing is a more efficient sense for processing information than sight. Some exercises can easily be presented on tape rather than in print. This variation can help reduce visual fatigue especially when texts contain long passages of narrative.

Many students with a visual impairment in Further and Higher Education rely heavily on tape recorders for activities such as taking notes and accessing information in books. Specially adapted tape recorders are commercially available and they range from handheld dictaphones to desktop variable-speed recorders capable of processing information at speeds well above the average silent reading rate for fully sighted adults. However the development of listening skills to this level requires careful training. Visual impairment brings no 'compensatory' increase in listening skills. In fact, there is some evidence to suggest that children with a visual impairment may have poorer listening skills than their classmates who are fully sighted.

Specific training in the development of listening skills is an essential part of the additional curriculum. This training needs to begin in the reception classes with the development of skills in identifying and discriminating between sounds. Many areas of the National Curriculum lend themselves easily to developing skills in listening. For example, in music lessons children can be encouraged to identify the sounds of different instruments or to reproduce sequences of notes or rhythms. Outside the classroom, opportunities can be taken to help children identify everyday sounds such as playground equipment and traffic noises. Commercial tapes or home-made tapes can provide practice in identifying noises which don't occur commonly in the school environment. Many elements of the National Literacy Strategy (NLS), such as listening to stories and identifying key characters and elements of the plot, help children to develop their listening skills. As children progress through the key stages they can be encouraged to make increasing use of listening skills to aid learning.

Touch

In order to access information, children with little or no vision will not only have to learn to make best use of their listening skills but will also need opportunities throughout their education to develop their sense of touch. The number of children in mainstream schools who rely upon hearing and touch as their main pathways for accessing the curriculum is relatively small, but is increasing as inclusion policies develop.

> Amy is educationally blind as a result of **retinopathy of prematurity**. She is in Year 8 in an inner-city comprehensive school where there is a specialist resource base for students with a visual impairment. She has enough residual vision to detect light and can point to the windows. She can detect the vague shape of people moving towards her in the corridor. She can identify bright colours very close to her right eye, but she cannot read print even when it is highly magnified. She has Braille versions of the main textbooks but work for some lessons has to be prepared in advance by the Braille technician in the Resource Centre. She is supported by a specialist teacher from the Resource Base in some lessons such as Science, PE and Maths.
>
> In some lessons she uses a laptop computer with speech software to record her work. At the start of each day she goes to the Resource Base to collect Braille versions of the worksheets for each lesson. At the end of each morning and afternoon session she downloads her work, producing print and Braille versions of the work she has done in lessons and puts the computer on charge. This morning she is visiting the Resource Base to collect a raised map she will need for the next geography lesson and to check that her taxi driver knows she will be staying late after school for her orchestra practice.

Like skills in listening, touch skills do not develop automatically in children who are blind. In the early stages of schooling, a primary aim will be to equip these children with the range of skills they will require to become efficient touch readers. They will need activities that will develop flexibility, dexterity and strength in their wrists and hands. They will need opportunities to develop light finger touch, line-tracking skills and skills in tactual perception, such as matching and discriminating textures and shapes.

In most respects the development of literacy for children who use Braille emerges from the same processes which shape the literacy of children who use print. All children need to use their knowledge of language and their experiences to predict meaning in their reading, but the preschool experiences of children with little or no sight are often different from those of their classmates. Like many children with low vision, they may have had fewer chances to explore their environment or to learn through incidental and unplanned experiences. They will not have had the opportunity to refine their motor skills by observing and copying the action of others and they will not have been exposed in the same way to the written word as it occurs incidentally in the environment. The child who is blind may have had little or no exposure to tactile books in the home.

The development of literacy in children who rely upon touch requires a range of activities designed to develop meaningful language based on first-hand concrete experiences. In the early stages of their schooling they will need opportunities to refine their motor skills, develop their touch perception and to learn in an atmosphere where their literacy achievements are recognised and valued.

The success of children who use Braille will depend to a great degree on the expertise in the teaching they receive. The Advisory Teacher of the visually impaired will normally be heavily involved with children who use Braille. However the day-to-day responsibility for the child's progress will fall upon the classroom teacher and the child's LSA.

It is likely that children who rely upon touch will require some individual teaching to develop their knowledge of the Braille code but the skills that they will need for touch reading can also be developed across the whole curriculum. For example, opportunities to work with plasticine or clay in art lessons can help to develop strength in the hands. Sorting and counting activities in maths can be used to help develop touch discrimination. Science provides the opportunity to explore by touch the different properties in materials such as their weight, hardness and texture. Activities in PE and games can help encourage coordination in gross and fine motor movements.

While the general sequence of the development of literacy in children who rely upon touch is the same as that of all children, they will need to learn different ways of accessing the written word. For almost a century Braille has been the dominant system of touch reading. Braille is based on a 'cell' of six raised dots arranged like the six on a domino.

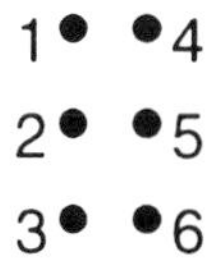

```
1●  ●4
2●  ●5
3●  ●6
```

Figure 4.2 The Braille cell

These 6 dots can be arranged into 63 different patterns and these patterns not only make up the alphabet and punctuation signs but are also used to create signs for whole words or groups of letters called 'contractions'.

There are two grades of British Braille. In Grade One Braille only the signs for the alphabet and punctuation are used. Grade Two Braille by comparison is a much more complex code in which words are written in a shorthand form. Grade Two Braille contains 189 contractions which include special signs for common combinations of letters such as, 'ed', 'er', 'ing', 'st', 'tion', 'ally', and 'ment'. There are special signs for frequently occurring words such as 'with', 'the', 'to', 'was', 'his'. There are also shortened forms of words such as 'gd' for 'good' and special signs to indicate numbers and capital letters. These contractions are governed by a complex system of 126 rules. Braille is a bulky medium and a standard print textbook at secondary school might take up several volumes when it is transcribed into Braille. Contracted Braille is necessary to save space and it also enables touch readers to read faster. The majority of touch reading materials published in the UK appear in Grade Two Braille and almost

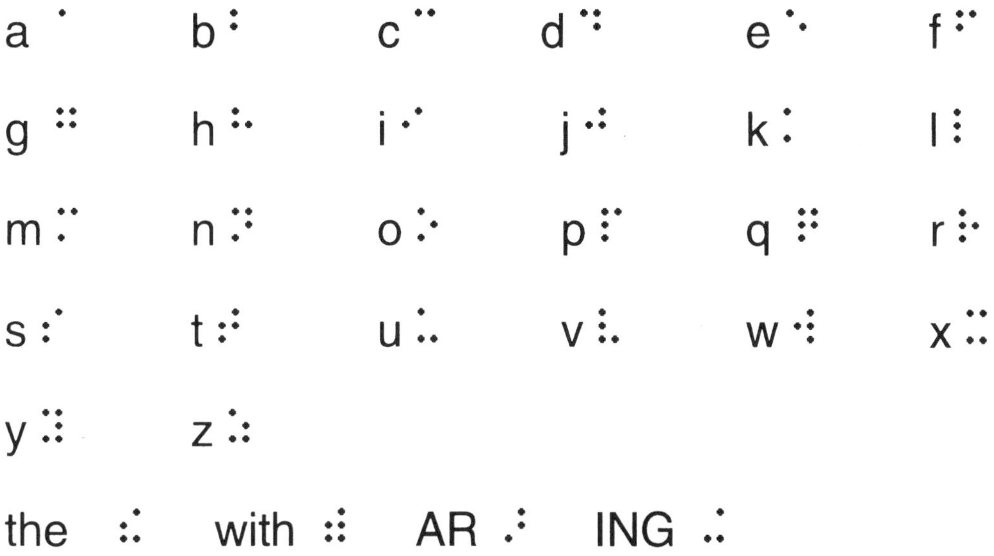

a ⠁   b ⠃   c ⠉   d ⠙   e ⠑   f ⠋

g ⠛   h ⠓   i ⠊   j ⠚   k ⠅   l ⠇

m ⠍   n ⠝   o ⠕   p ⠏   q ⠟   r ⠗

s ⠎   t ⠞   u ⠥   v ⠧   w ⠺   x ⠭

y ⠽   z ⠵

the ⠮   with ⠾   AR ⠜   ING ⠬

Figure 4.3 Braille – the letters of the alphabet and four common contractions

all children are taught to read using reading schemes that introduce contracted Grade Two Braille from the start.

The NLS is changing some of the approaches to the teaching of reading among children who use Braille in mainstream primary schools. There is general agreement that children who use Braille should be included in the Literacy Hour but some of the techniques such as the use of 'big books' for whole-class teaching will require adaptation to enable the Braille reader to participate. There are fundamental differences between the processes of reading through touch and through sight which will affect the teaching approaches. For example, while the eye can easily take in a whole word at a glance, the finger can only take in one character at a time. This letter-by-letter approach in Braille reading means that children who use Braille will rely heavily on phonic approaches rather than whole-word recognition or 'Look and Say' methods in the early stages.

Obviously, in the early stages the Advisory Teacher of the visually impaired will be closely involved in decisions about how the NLS can be adapted for the child who uses Braille. However, regular specialist input will be necessary and pupils' mechanical skills and knowledge of the Braille code will need to be monitored and assessed at both primary and secondary level. At the appropriate stages the child will need to be taught the specialist Braille codes for writing mathematics, chemistry, music, and foreign languages.

The development of skills in reading and writing through Braille is a key part of the entitlement of children who are blind and well-developed Braille skills are essential if the child is to be able to access the curriculum.

Braille writing

Most children who write through Braille begin by using a mechanical Braille writer called the 'Perkins'. This has six-keys, each corresponding to a dot in the Braille cell. When the keys are pressed down in the appropriate combination, raised letters are embossed onto a sheet of manilla paper which is fed manually into the machine.

In recent years a variety of electronic Braille-writing devices have become available which also use six-key input. Output may take the form of speech or a renewable tactile display on the front of the machine. Most of these machines can store information which can then be translated into print and downloaded to a conventional printer.

As with most children with a severe visual impairment in mainstream schools, Braille users will usually be taught to touch-type using a conventional QWERTY keyboard. They will use a conventional laptop or desktop computer with adapted software and record and retrieve information using synthesised speech. Most

Figure 4.4 Using a Perkins brailler

older children will be able to provide their class teacher with text work in print by using appropriate adaptive technology, but in some subjects (such as maths) work will be completed on a Perkins mechanical Brailler and will need to be transcribed into print and this task is often the responsibility of the LSA or specialist teacher.

In mainstream schools where there is a specialist Resource Base for children with a visual impairment there may be a specially employed technician who will be responsible for the preparation of tactile materials. Where support is available for the preparation of adapted materials, the class teacher obviously needs to provide the information well in advance about the books, handouts, diagrams and maps that will be required during lessons. In situations where individual children who are blind are in mainstream schools where there is no specialist

Resource Base, the need for advanced consultation with the specialist teacher becomes even more important.

The class teacher has a responsibility to ensure that the child with a visual impairment has equal access to information in the classroom. Awareness of the needs of children and the media they use can help the class teacher to work successfully with the child and to coordinate the support available to achieve equality of opportunity.

Recommended reading

Arter, C. (1997) 'Listening skills', in Mason, H., McCall, S. *et al. Visual Impairment: Access to Education for Children and Young People*. London: David Fulton Publishers.

Arter, C., McCall, S. and Bowyer, T. (1996) 'Handwriting and children with a visual impairment.' *British Journal of Special Education* **23**(1), 25–29.

McCall, S. (1997) 'The development of literacy through touch', in Mason, H., McCall, S. *et al. Visual Impairment: Access to Education for Children and Young People*, London: David Fulton Publishers.

Wormsley, D. P. and De Andrea, F. M. (1997) *Instructional Strategies for Braille Literacy.* New York: American Foundation for the Blind.

CHAPTER 5

Learning to be independent

Juliet Stone

One of the major challenges facing a child or young person with a visual impairment is that of learning to be independent. Without clear sight most of the everyday tasks, which people who are fully sighted take for granted, become very difficult. Even a seemingly simple activity, such as making a cup of coffee using boiling water, is fraught with difficulties. Being as independent as possible is important for all of us, and children who are fully sighted learn many skills which lead to independence by copying their parents and other people. For children with severe visual impairment, learning skills through imitation is not possible. They may have to be taught how to move independently around the environment and how to cook, clean and care for themselves. This chapter will deal firstly with the teaching of mobility and orientation to children with a visual impairment, and will then discuss aspects of other independence skills.

Mobility and orientation

The ways in which people with severe visual impairments get around safely are well known. We have all seen people who are visually impaired using a long white cane, a guide dog or being guided around by another person. All of these methods have advantages and disadvantages and it is important that children and young people are assessed to find the particular approach which will suit them best. Young children initially rely on the help of a sighted adult or peer and gradually get used to using other methods.

It is probably easy to understand why children who are blind should have difficulties in moving around safely, but children who have reduced vision may also need support.

> Katy, a seven year old child, has **photophobia**, which means that she finds bright light painful and disabling. On a dull-weather day, she finds her way around the playground easily, but on a bright sunny day, the outside area is a large expanse

of glare and she is unable to see anything. The variability in her vision causes her difficulties and staff who are unaware of her particular condition are confused.

Simon, on the other hand has **macula degeneration**; an effect of this is poor depth perception. He is unable to identify stairs, kerbs and any changes in walking surfaces, often confusing a shadow on the ground for a large obstacle. Both of these children have difficulties in moving around safely.

Terminology

There are two aspects to being able to travel independently. The first of these is to be able to move around without bumping into obstacles or tripping over kerbs or steps and this is usually referred to as 'mobility'.

The other aspect is called 'orientation' and this is all about children knowing where they are, where they are going and how they are going to get there. This can be very difficult, especially for the child who has never seen clearly. How does a child know how to get from the classroom to the secretary's office? The child has to learn the route bit by bit, memorising any left or right turns, until the whole route can be managed. This route-building becomes far more difficult, of course, outside the school and in a wider environment. Orientation takes a long time to master and it is a concept where support staff can have an important part to play in helping children understand their environment and to learn routes within it.

Mobility teaching

The teaching of orientation and mobility is usually delivered by a mobility specialist. These specialists may be employed by the special school for children with visual impairments or the advisory service which supports the mainstream school. Sometimes the Education Department will buy in the time of a mobility specialist from the local Social Services. Children with severe visual impairments may have up to three lessons per week, depending on their need and the availability of the mobility specialist. Other children may have only one lesson a week or less. Whatever level of teaching they are receiving it is still a very short amount of time and so it is clearly important that the mobility programme is supported by the school staff throughout the rest of the week and there are several ways in which this can be done.

There are many areas of the curriculum which can promote the learning of mobility and orientation skills. In Geography for example, children are able to study the locality and learn map-reading skills. In PE children are usually able to develop skills in free movement and improve their stamina. Mathematics can also develop relevant skills. The ability to estimate distance is very useful in mobility and the study of measurement and speed can help in this. Children and young people need to have a certain level of assertiveness and drama can be used to help develop children's self-presentation skills and their confidence, which will be needed when travelling independently.

One of the most important ways teachers can support a mobility programme is to present children with opportunities which help them overcome their reluctance to travel independently. It can feel too dangerous and it takes a lot of effort and concentration. Giving young children errands around the primary school, such as fetching and returning registers, can help to develop their self-confidence in travelling by themselves. The school day will provide many other such opportunities. In the secondary phase, the young people are likely to be moving around a larger school site, which in itself will promote mobility skills and the training they receive at this time will probably include trips to the local shopping centre and the use of public transport. When children change schools, such as at the time of transfer from primary to secondary school, they will need to have time to learn the new campus and the routes within it.

Close collaboration between the mobility specialist and the rest of the staff can ensure that the staff know which stage of the programme the child has reached and which specific skills are currently being taught. Staff can then support children in establishing and practising these particular skills. Perhaps the mobility specialist has just taught the child the route from the classroom to a new part of the school and practising this with adult support will be most helpful.

All staff should know how to guide children with visual impairment to ensure their safety and training in guidance techniques can be requested from the mobility specialist. The main principle to remember is that the person guiding must ensure that the walking space of the child being guided is clear, and free from any obstacles. This takes a certain amount of concentration, but it is essential that children can totally trust the people guiding them.

Children and young people will also require training in the routes around their homes as well as the routes between home and school.

Daily living skills

Being able to look after yourself and your possessions involves a whole range of different skills, from personal grooming and hygiene to caring for clothes and preparing food. Children and young people with visual impairment need time to learn these skills and also time to practise them so that they become part of their daily routine. Teaching these skills requires a systematic and orderly approach and tasks must be taught through a step-by-step method. For example, consider the activity of making a sandwich. Equipment and materials, such as the knife and plate, bread and butter must be organised so that they are in reach, but placed safely. The child will then have to learn to position the bread on the plate, put the butter and then the spread on it so that the bread is evenly covered, and finally learn how to cut the sandwich safely. Each time this task is taught, the equipment should be set in the same place and the steps to complete the task must be the same. In addition, the 'teacher' should use the same language and terminology.

Young children will begin with the basic skills of dressing, feeding and toileting, all of which can be daunting if you do not see clearly or at all. In the initial stages, clothes can be chosen which make the task easier, such as coats with zips rather than buttons and slip-on shoes rather than ones with laces. This is not a long-term solution as young people will want to acquire fashion clothes with all types of fastening and each of these will have to be taught.

As they move into school, children will need to learn how to eat appropriately, using a knife and fork. Some people with severe visual impairments may find managing the eating of some foods difficult. For example, when eating in public places, children may need advice about which meals are easily manageable.

Children will also need to be learning such skills as pouring liquids and handling equipment. As they get older and move into adolescence, they will need other skills such as shopping, cooking and ways of labelling and storing ingredients. In class they will need to be encouraged to develop organisational skills so that they always know where things are and it is essential that staff supporting children with visual impairments follow this principle. Any labels will need to be appropriate for the individual child's level of vision.

> Shabina, aged fifteen, is very fashion conscious and loves clothes. She has very limited sight and now has little colour vision due to **optic atrophy**. She has to find a way to label her clothes, so that she does not put clashing colours together, unless she wishes to do so.

Other young people will want to know ways in which they can label their CDs and tapes.

Adolescence also brings the need for more sophisticated skills in the area of personal hygiene. These include washing the hair, shaving and putting on makeup. If young people are preparing to go to college, or to leave home to live independently, they will need to be thoroughly efficient in all of these tasks.

The importance of early education

The teaching of life skills needs to begin early. It can be very difficult to motivate older children to look after themselves if they have got used to having everything done for them. If parents receive appropriate support and information when their children are very young, they will be able to teach them basic independence skills such as dressing and feeding and will encourage them to move around the house by themselves. Parents will always need to consider the safety aspects, but hopefully they will realise that their children need to get used to a certain amount of bumps and bruises and learn to pick themselves up and try again. However, it can sometimes be a real burden for busy parents to find the time first to teach and then allow children to carry out these skills. It is so much quicker to dress or feed children oneself than to wait for them to do it themselves. This means that many children come to school without having mastered these things. Time in a busy timetable may need to be found and staff support given to the children as they learn these basic skills.

Fortunately, many play activities are ideal situations. For example, the child playing at the water table and pouring water from one container to another is setting the basis for making a cup of tea in later life. The dressing-up corner and play house also provide opportunities to practise these skills.

Conclusion

It is important to remember that any lessening of dependence is a step towards independence. It does not matter how far children are able to achieve the goals of independent living as long as they are helped to realise their own individual potential. Children with additional disabilities will clearly not be able to reach the levels that other children do. However, many children learn to become fully independent adults, able to take advantage of employment opportunities and to live totally fulfilling lives.

Recommended reading

Royal National Institute for the Blind (in association with Guide Dogs for the Blind Association) (1987) *How to Guide a Blind Person.* London: RNIB.
Stone, J. (1995) *Mobility for Special Needs.* London: Cassell.

CHAPTER 6

The child with a visual impairment in combination with additional difficulties

Mike McLinden

Introduction

Recent national surveys suggest that children with a visual impairment can be broadly divided into two distinct groups, a group of children with a visual impairment and no additional difficulties, and a *larger* group who have a visual impairment in combination with a range of additional difficulties (e.g. Walker *et al.* 1992). While the overall population of children with a visual impairment appears to be more or less constant, the proportion of pupils with additional disabilities within this population is forecast to increase. This increase can be partly linked to recent improvements in medical knowledge and techniques which have resulted in a changing pattern in the medical conditions of children entering the education system. For example, improved medical expertise and Special Baby Care Units for premature babies have resulted in many babies who are born with complications surviving today who would not have previously survived infancy. Similarly, improvements in medical screening techniques and genetic counselling have resulted in fewer cases of children being born with visual impairments that were once more common within the population.

The majority of children who have a visual impairment in combination with additional difficulties are currently being educated in special schools for the blind and schools for children with severe learning difficulties. In line with recent legislation however, an increasing proportion may receive at least part of their education within the mainstream environment. This chapter offers an introduction to the educational needs created by a visual impairment in combination with additional difficulties, and considers relevant factors in addressing these needs. It is written in a different style from that adopted in the text thus far, in that the reader is asked to use the information gathered in previous chapters to reflect on the particular issues raised in relation to three case studies, each selected to highlight the wide range of educational needs within the population.

Setting the scene

The scenario presented below provides an opportunity to begin reflecting on what classroom life might be like for a child with a visual impairment in combination with additional difficulties who is placed in a mainstream classroom environment.

Shan

Shan is a Year 3 pupil who has recently transferred from a special school for children with a visual impairment to a local mainstream primary school. Shan has restricted use of her legs and is reliant on others to push her wheelchair. She has a severe visual impairment which means that, even with her glasses, it is difficult for her to see very much detail at a distance. Shan has good understanding of language but frequently gets frustrated as other people do not always under-stand her attempts to express herself. Although Shan is in Key Stage 2 she is still working at Level 1 in the core National Curriculum subjects and follows an adapted curriculum. She is supported in class by a full time LSA. Shan enjoys her time at school but does feel that events happen very quickly in class and wishes that sometimes an activity could be repeated to provide her with a better opportunity to understand what has happened.

Consider now what particular educational needs might be created within this situation and how those responsible for Shan's education might best meet these needs. For example, how will others know where to stand so that Shan is able to see them clearly? How best can she be encouraged to join in with the group discussion? How can activities be arranged to provide her with opportunities to join in with other children? How might opportunities be provided for her to gain a better understanding of what is happening during the course of the day? How might the teacher provide her with appropriately challenging work to meet the requirements of the National Curriculum?

Although presented as an imaginary scenario, the situation described for Shan may well be a very real one for an increasing number of children with a visual impairment in combination with additional difficulties who receive at least part of their education within a mainstream classroom environment. Three such children are now introduced as case studies for you to consider further.

Saquib

Saquib is a 10-year-old boy who is diagnosed as having cerebral palsy. In addi-tion to wearing glasses to correct a refractive error (**hypermetropia**), Saquib has **strabismus (**squint). He tends to adopt an abnormal head posture and his work needs to be carefully positioned for him to see it clearly. Saquib has always had limited independent mobility and relies on an electric wheelchair to move around the class environment. It was felt that Saquib would benefit from a mainstream school environment and in accordance with the wishes of his parents he transferred from a special school for children with a visual impairment to his local primary school at the age of 8 years. Saquib is working at Level 2 in English, Maths and Science. He is on medication for epilepsy which affects his level of arousal and his ability to work in the classroom during the day. He receives regular input from a range of professionals including the Visual Impairment Advisory Service and is supported on a full-time basis by an LSA.

Julie

Julie is a young girl of 8 years of age who attends her local primary school. Following a road accident at the age of six she lost all useful vision in her left eye. Her right eye was also damaged and although she retains some useful vision for orientation and mobility she has difficulty in using her vision for close-up work. In addition there was significant damage to her dominant right hand and she now has only restricted movement. Julie appears to be falling significantly behind her peers in her academic progress and is still working at Level 1 in English, Maths and Science. Despite the introduction of a CCTV, Julie shows only a limited interest in learning to read and is not able to consistently recognise her name or the letters of the alphabet. The Advisory Teacher of the Visually Impaired supports Julie for one hour a day in the classroom. He is using a range of activities to develop her tactual skills and is considering introducing the Moon code[1] as her reading medium.

Jamie

Jamie is a 7-year-old child with Down's Syndrome who has recently started attending his local primary school on a one day a week placement. During the rest of the week he attends a special school for children with severe learning difficulties. Jamie has high **myopia** in both eyes and needs to wear glasses throughout the school day. He has a full-time LSA who supports him in both school environments. Jamie uses objects of reference[2] during the school day to help him understand the structure of his day. These are real objects which can be used to represent a particular activity or person. For example, a paintbrush is used to represent Art and Jamie carries this object to the Art activity. Jamie is beginning to recognise familiar letters in simple texts and is using his knowledge of letters and sound–symbol relationships in order to establish meaning. He is currently working within Level 1 in all three core subjects. The placement has been considered a success and it will be recommended at his Annual Review that it be increased to two days a week.

---

[1] Moon is tactile code which is based on the Roman alphabet. Although it has traditionally been used by adults who have lost their vision later in life, more recently it has been used as an alternative to Braille for children with a visual impairment in combination with additional difficulties. A summary of the Moon alphabet is provided in Figure 6.1. Further information about Moon can be obtained from the RNIB.

[2] Objects of reference are objects or part of objects which can be used to represent a particular activity or person. They are commonly used in developing early communication skills for children with a visual impairment in combination with a range of additional difficulties. See the Recommended Reading section for more information.

These case studies provide a summary of three very different children and serve to illustrate their wide range of educational needs. In order to feel confident in welcoming a child with a visual impairment in combination with additional difficulties into the mainstream classroom the teacher will need to be aware of:

- the educational implications that may be created by a visual impairment in combination with additional difficulties;
- the implications for planning and delivery of the Curriculum (including the National Curriculum);
- relevant factors in the design and management of an appropriate learning environment to address these needs.

These areas are explored further below, with opportunities provided for the reader to reflect on the implications of the visual impairment in combination with additional difficulties for each child presented in the case studies.

Educational implications

What is the cause and age of onset of the visual impairment?

Knowing the cause and age of onset of the condition is important when considering the educational implications of a visual impairment for a child. Basic information will be available in the child's files, and further advice should always be sought from the local Visual Impairment Advisory Service.

A broad distinction can be made between a visual impairment which affects the eyes (ocular visual impairment), and an impairment which affects the visual processing parts of the brain (cortical visual impairment or cerebral visual dysfunction). The educational implications of these conditions are very different and require quite different management programmes.

A further distinction can be made between a condition that a child is born with and one that is acquired after birth. For example, Saquib suffers from a congenital condition which is not a disease and was not inherited. He was deprived of oxygen for a significant period of time during birth and was diagnosed with cerebral palsy, a condition which results in impaired motor control and is frequently linked with disorders of vision and hearing.

Jamie has Down's Syndrome, a hereditary condition caused by a chromosomal abnormality with clear distinguishing physical features. A range of visual abnormalities are linked with Down's Syndrome including **strabismus** (squints) and high refractive errors, (i.e. **myopia** and **hypermetropia**). Many children in this population have significant developmental delay and will require specialist educational provision.

Julie has an acquired or adventitious condition. She had a normal childhood for the first five years of her life, until she was seriously injured in a road accident. Although she suffered a number of disabling injuries it was not thought at the time that there was any lasting damage to her brain and her parents were keen for her to return to her local school. Her increasing developmental delay is a source of concern however and her school placement is being reviewed.

What might be the impact of a visual impairment in combination with additional difficulties on the child's early development?

Much of a young child's learning is incidental with vision being used to link the information received from each of the other senses. A visual impairment serves to restrict both the *quantity* and *quality* of information available and can affect the child's ability to understand and organise images of the world. On its own this may result in developmental delay during the first few years of life; in combination with additional difficulties the impact of this restriction is frequently more pronounced.

Consider first the possible impact of a visual impairment in combination with additional difficulties for Saquib and Jamie's early understanding of the world.

> Saquib was never observed independently reaching out to grasp a toy and even when placed in his hand there was minimal exploration of objects. Much of his learning was based on 'hand-over-hand' activities within which an adult directed the movements of his hands. His difficulties in moving his head quickly to track a moving object meant that he was often unable to watch the movement of others.
>
> Jamie was provided with a rich learning environment when growing up, with specialist input from a range of professionals. He was encouraged to actively explore a variety of different objects and to compensate for his visual impairment these were often brought close to his eyes for more detailed observation. Jamie had a relatively limited period of concentration and was rarely observed playing independently with toys.

Compare each of these descriptions with that of Julie who did not lose her vision until a later age. Julie was a lively and active infant, keen to independently explore and find out about objects in her world. You may wish to reflect on how Saquib and Jamie's early understanding of the world would have been different from that of Julie at similar stages during their early development, and to consider the implications of this for planning and delivery of an appropriate curriculum.

Planning and delivery of the curriculum

How might the results of a visual assessment assist the teacher in planning the curriculum for a child?

Knowledge of the way a child uses his or her vision (visual function) will be important to the teacher in planning the curriculum and details relating to visual assessment are provided in Chapter 2. When additional difficulties are present however, it can be difficult to accurately assess a child's visual function through standard clinical assessment, and the teacher will also need to consider the findings of a functional visual assessment.

To determine Saquib's use of vision, for example, it was necessary to consider carefully both his head and body position as well as his level of arousal at the time of assessment. Although a clinical assessment offered some useful information regarding his visual acuity, of particular value to the class teacher were the findings of the functional vision assessment which highlighted how Saquib actually used his vision within a particular setting in the classroom, i.e. when sitting by the window on a sunny day.

Assessment of Jamie's vision took place within the classroom environment, as his responses within a clinical setting were not consistent. This assessment was used to determine the print size for his reading as well as an appropriate seating position for his class work.

A clinical assessment shows that Julie does not have sufficient vision to read print without the use of an LVA and the tactile code Moon (see Figure 6.1) is currently being considered for her reading medium. A functional visual assessment has been carried out to determine how she uses her vision for independent orientation and mobility within the school environment.

What might be the implications of the visual impairment in combination with additional difficulties for planning and delivering the National Curriculum?

Many children with a visual impairment in combination with additional difficulties continue to function at an earlier stage of development than their sighted peers throughout their education. Consider for example Jamie, who at the age of 7 is still working within Level 1 in the three core National Curriculum subjects.

∧	ᘈ	⊂	⊃	⌐	⌐	∩	o			ᒍ
a	b	c	d	e	f	g	h	i	j
<	L	¬	N	O	ᗯ	ᗰ	\	/	—
k	l	m	n	o	p	q	r	s	t
∪	V	∩	>	⌐	Z				
u	v	w	x	y	z				

Figure 6.1   Summary of the Moon Alphabet

This has particular implications for Jamie's teacher in planning and delivering the National Curriculum to enable Jamie to progress, i.e. to gain in knowledge, understanding and skills, and to demonstrate achievement.

Jamie's opportunities for incidental learning will be significantly reduced as a result of his visual impairment. He therefore requires an adapted programme which provides opportunities for him to demonstrate progression and achievement in his learning and which is incorporated within a carefully structured learning environment.

Read Jamie's case study again. Consider then what adaptations you, as Jamie's class teacher, might make in your planning and delivery of a Key Stage 1 programme of study in Reading to allow Jamie to demonstrate progression with appropriately challenging work. What adaptations will be required in order for Jamie to access this programme? For example, how appropriate will the use of labels on the classroom walls be to Jamie as a way of reinforcing his learning, given his reduced distance vision? How else might information be presented to him in a more appropriate way?

Design and management of the learning environment

What factors need to be considered in the design and management of the learning environment?

In addressing the particular educational needs created by a visual impairment in combination with additional difficulties, the classroom teacher, with support from the local Visual Impairment Advisory Service, will need to carefully assess the learning environment to ensure that it is appropriate for a child. Many of the important areas to consider in managing the learning environment for a child with a visual impairment are presented in Chapters 2 and 3. A number of additional aspects, which relate particularly to the child with additional difficulties, are summarised in Figure 6.2.

You might wish to explore these areas further in relation to your own classroom environment (or one you are familiar with), and consider what adaptations might be required in order to meet the needs of one of the children described in the case studies. For example, what adaptations might be required to enable Saquib to see work on the wall displays from his wheelchair height? Would Julie be able to independently locate the girls' toilet or would more appropriate signs need to be installed on the door? How would the arrival or departure of visitors be announced to ensure that Jamie knows who is in the classroom during a particular activity?

It will also be necessary to consider how you as the class teacher might review on a regular basis the extent to which the learning environment is appropriate in

Design and management of the mainstream learning environment for a child with a visual impairment in combination with additional difficulties

Journey to class

- To what extent is the child able to find the classroom independently on arrival at school? What particular distinguishing features might be of value, (e.g. enlarged high contrast letters or tactile symbols on the class door)?
- Are any words or symbols used outside the classroom positioned at an appropriate height for a child?
- Are there any obstacles which may prevent a safe passage for the child's journey to and within the classroom?
- To what extent is the child able to independently locate his or her working area on arrival in class?

Participation in class

- To what extent is the child aware of who is in the classroom during a particular session? How, for example, is the arrival and departure of visitors announced?
- What possible distractions are there for the child during a lesson, (e.g. noise from the playground or corridor)? How might this affect his or her seating position during the lesson?
- To what extent is the child provided with opportunities to interact with other children during class time?
- To what extent is the child provided with opportunities to be included in class decisions and discussion?
- How aware are the other children in the class of the child's special educational needs?
- How is the child made aware of any changes that are made within the classroom, (e.g. changes to wall displays)?
- To what extent is the child able to anticipate when one session ends and another begins?
- To what extent does the child understand his or her timetable for each day? Would a picture timetable or 'tactile calendar' based on objects of reference be useful to aid this understanding?
- To what extent is the child able to independently make a request, for example, to go to the toilet?

Journey between activities/classes

- What opportunities can be provided to ensure that the child understands what activity he or she is going to next? Would it be useful for the child to carry a symbol, e.g. a picture or an 'object of reference', between classes?
- To what extent can a journey between activities/classes be made independently? What opportunities can be provided to increase independent orientation and mobility?
- Is it possible to phase departure from an activity session to provide additional time for the child to find his or her way to the next session?

Figure 6.2   Design and management of the mainstream learning environment

helping to meet the child's educational needs. As part of this review it will be useful for the teacher (as well as children in the class!) to participate in a range of visual awareness activities. By wearing special spectacles designed to 'simulate' a particular visual condition (available from the local Visual Impairment Advisory Service), it is possible to raise awareness of the child's particular perspective within the class. Activities might be structured to include: arrival into the classroom, participation in a lesson, joining in with a class discussion and departure from the classroom.

Concluding thoughts

Children with a visual impairment in combination with additional disabilities present a special challenge to professionals responsible for their education. Although they may work closely with other professionals, teachers in a mainstream classroom will need to have knowledge of the particular educational needs created by the unique combination of the child's difficulties, as well as an understanding of how best these needs can be addressed within an appropriate learning environment. The information presented in this chapter can only provide an introduction to this area and the teacher seeking more detailed information is referred to the Recommended reading section.

Recommended reading

Aitkens, S. and Buultjens, M. (1992) *Vision for Doing. Assessing Functional Vision of Learners who are Multiply Disabled.* Edinburgh: Moray House.

Ockleford, A. (1994) *Objects of Reference: Promoting Communication Skills and Concept Development for Visually Impaired Children who have other Disabilities.* London: RNIB.

Rogow, S. M. (1988) *Helping the Visually Impaired Child with Developmental Problems.* New York: Teachers' College Press.

McLinden, M. (1997) 'Children with multiple disabilities and a visual impairment', in Mason, H., McCall, S. *et al.* (eds) *Visual Impairment: Access to Education for Children and Young People.* London: David Fulton Publishers.

VITAL/RNIB (1998) Approaches to Working with Children with Multiple Disabilities and a Visual Impairment. London: RNIB.

CHAPTER 7

Final thoughts

The future

Education is at a crossroads. Changes are taking place within special education as government and society increasingly acknowledge that children and young people with special educational needs and their parents have the right to be involved in making decisions about educational placements. Attendance at a local mainstream school is now often the preferred choice and schools will be required to adopt fully-inclusive practices which meet the needs of these pupils.

The new trends in education have major implications for the role of teachers in both mainstream and special school settings.

Teachers in mainstream schools will increasingly be expected to teach pupils with a range of special needs and to work as part of a collaborative multi-disciplinary team. Government initiatives, such as the National Literacy Strategy (Literacy Hour), already require teachers to work more flexibly with other professionals and parents. Recent proposals from the Teacher Training Agency (TTA) recognise that there is a need for continuing training as part of 'life-long' professional development to equip teachers with these new skills.

Teachers in special schools for the visually impaired are also witnessing changes. At present pupils within these schools are more likely to have complex special needs in combination with their visual impairment. The Green Paper (DfEE 1997) suggests that special schools will develop a role as regional resource centres and special school staff may be used as outreach advisers to work with mainstream colleagues.

The authors firmly believe that teachers working with children and young people who have a visual impairment should have access to a qualified specialist teacher of the visually impaired. There is a long tradition of training specialist teachers in this area and for the foreseeable future a specialist qualification will remain a mandatory requirement when teaching groups of pupils with a visual impairment. A specialist teacher will be able to advise those mainstream teachers who are interested in further training in this challenging and highly rewarding area of special needs teaching.

Further information

It is hoped that this book has provided teachers in mainstream schools, who are new to teaching children and young people with a visual impairment, with some basic understanding of the needs of this group of pupils. For those wishing to find out more, the additional texts cited as recommended reading will prove invaluable. In addition, a number of useful addresses are provided.

There is an ever-increasing amount of interesting material available on the World Wide Web and readers are referred to:

Lea Hyvarinen's resource pages:
http: //med-aapos.bu.edu/leaweb/index.html

Royal National Institute for the Blind:
http: //www.rnib.org.uk/

Scottish Sensory Service:
http: //www.ssc.mhie.ac.uk/

Useful addresses

RNIB (Royal National Institute for the Blind)
224 Great Portland Street
London W1N 6AA

Tel: 0171 388 1266

VIEW (formerly the Association for the Education and Welfare of the Visually Impaired) contact:

Mary Foulstone
Royal National College
College Road
Hereford HR1 1EB

Tel: 01432 265 725

Research Centre for the Education of the Visually Handicapped (RCEVH)
The School of Education
University of Birmingham
Edgbaston
Birmingham B15 2TT

Tel: 0121 414 4866

Diagram of the eye

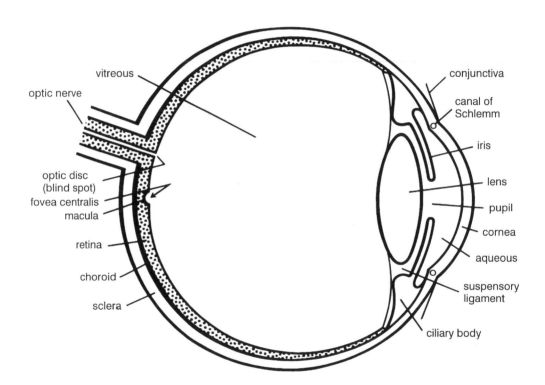

vitreous

optic nerve

optic disc
(blind spot)

fovea centralis

macula

retina

choroid

sclera

conjunctiva

canal of
Schlemm

iris

lens

pupil

cornea

aqueous

suspensory
ligament

ciliary body

Glossary

accommodate
The adjustment of the eye for seeing at different distances by changing the shape of the lens through the action of the ciliary muscle.

albinism
A hereditary loss of pigment in the iris, skin and hair, usually associated with lower visual acuity, *nystagmus* and *photophobia*.

cataracts
A condition in which the lens of the eye becomes opaque.

hypermetropia
A refractive error in which the rays of light come to a focus behind the retina (long-sightedness).

macular degeneration
A central degenerative condition affecting the most sensitive part of the retina, the macula.

myopia
A refractive error in which the rays of light come to a focus in front of the retina (short-sightedness).

nystagmus
An involuntary, rapid movement of the eyeball.

optic atrophy
Degeneration of the optic nerve.

photophobia
Abnormal sensitivity to, and discomfort from, light.

retinoblastoma
A cancerous tumour of the retina in infants.

retinitis pigmentosa
A group of hereditary conditions affecting the retina and characterised by pigment changes.

retinopathy of prematurity
A disease of the retina which chiefly occurs in infants born prematurely and who received excessive oxygen.

strabismus
Failure of the two eyes to simultaneously direct their gaze at the same object (squint).

References

Arter, C. and Mason, H. (1994) 'Spelling for the visually impaired child', *British Journal of Visual Impairment* **12**(2), 18–21.

Clunies-Ross, L. and Franklin, A. (1997) 'Where have all the children gone? An analysis of the new statistical data on visual impairment amongst children in England, Scotland and Wales'. *British Journal of Visual Impairment,* **15**(2), 48–53.

Department for Education (DfE) (1994) *Code of Practice on the Identification and Assessment of Special Educational Needs.* London: Central Office of Information.

Department for Education and Employment (DfEE) (1997) *Excellence for all Children: Meeting Special Educational Needs.* London: HMSO.

Mason, H., McCall, S. *et al.* (1997) *Visual Impairment: Access to Education for Children and Young People.* London: David Fulton Publishers.

Walker, E., Tobin, M., McKennell, A. (1992) *Blind and Partially Sighted Children in Britain: the RNIB Survey. Volume 2.* London: HMSO.